# PROSE PAPERS

# PROSE PAPERS

BY
JOHN DRINKWATER

*Essay Index Reprint Series*

 BOOKS FOR LIBRARIES PRESS
FREEPORT, NEW YORK

First Published 1917
Reprinted 1969

STANDARD BOOK NUMBER:
8369-1205-5

LIBRARY OF CONGRESS CATALOG CARD NUMBER:
70-90631

PRINTED IN THE UNITED STATES OF AMERICA

# DEDICATION

My dear William Rothenstein,

I dedicate these essays to you, first for the profound pleasure that your drawings have given me, and in homage to an art the contemplation of which is a daily and growing inspiration to my own life and work. Then, it is to thank you for having found for me a corner of your enchanted Cotswold country. Lastly, and, perhaps, chiefly, it is in admiration for a generosity to your fellow-painters that is as heartening as it seems, unhappily, to be rare. I do not know whether my own experience of literary life has been uncommonly fortunate: fortunate it certainly has been. The chivalry that I have found in writers of an older generation than myself has only been a less intimate delight than the fellowship of my immediate contemporaries. With many of the Georgian poets, my collaborators in *New Numbers* and others, I have formed close friendships, and I know of nothing more splendid than the way in which these men, with various and often violently opposing views about their art, realise that they all are working for a common end, and are enthusiastic one for another's success—allowing always, of course, a resentment of dishonest work. Among painters of my own generation, and I am told that it is not a new phenomenon, I have not observed the same good-will. I have observed, rather, a disposition to intolerance, sometimes to jealousy. What the reason may be I do not know. Whether it is that the painter's emotion is, by the nature of his art, less tempered with philosophy than the poet's, or whether the rivalry of school-life makes for friction, I cannot say. But, whatever the cause, the effect is lamentable. If an artist, in any kind, does honest work, making no concessions from his vision, he is a fool if he expects anything more from the public than a slowly mellowing antagonism; but that his spirit should be impoverished in its struggle—for these things are impoverishing, however proud the denial may be—by the disparagement of his fellow-artists, or that he in turn should be ungenerous to men whose brave intention is his own, is ugly and distressing. We artists have the world to fight. Prejudice, indifference, positive hostility, misrepresentation, a total failure to understand the purposes and the power of art, beset us on every side. Nevertheless, if the world is to be renewed, it will be renewed by us, and with a sense of this responsibility upon us it is something meaner than folly to waste our energies in quarrelling among ourselves.

It is to the magnanimity with which, in your actions and your utterances, you have witnessed against this illiberality, that I wish to pay tribute in this dedication. Nothing in the public affairs of art has been more inspiriting in my time than the tributes that you have paid to your contemporaries, and your eager recognition of the painters of a new generation, some of them in revolt against the methods of your own art. Your illustrious distinction as a creator gives peculiar dignity to this generosity of mind, and I am, as everyone who cares for the health of art must be,

Very gratefully yours,<br>JOHN DRINKWATER.

FAR OAKRIDGE,
*September*, 1917.

## NOTE

THESE papers, varied in occasion, have, nevertheless, a common theme. They consider many writers, but in all of them, I hope, will be found a governing conception of the art with which they are concerned.

For leave to reprint some of them I thank Messrs. J. M. Dent & Sons, Ltd., Messrs. George Routledge & Sons, Ltd., and Mr. Martin Secker; also the Editors of *The British Review*, *The Contemporary Review*, *The Journal of English Studies*, *The Manchester Guardian*, *The Nation*, *The Nineteenth Century* and *The World*. The paper on Rupert Brooke has already appeared in a small privately printed edition.

# CONTENTS

| | PAGE |
|---|---|
| POETRY AND CONDUCT | 11 |
| THE VALUE OF POETRY IN EDUCATION | 35 |
| THE POET AND HIS VISION | 48 |
| ART AND THE ARTIST | 58 |
| CHAUCER: THE POET OF SPRING | 66 |
| PHILIP SIDNEY | 74 |
| THOMAS GRAY | 94 |
| S. T. COLERIDGE | 109 |
| THE BRONTËS AS POETS | 118 |
| FREDERICK TENNYSON | 131 |
| WILLIAM MORRIS AND THE STATE | 138 |
| THEODORE WATTS-DUNTON | 147 |
| RUPERT BROOKE | 174 |
| RUPERT BROOKE ON JOHN WEBSTER | 193 |
| THE NATURE OF DRAMA | 199 |
| ST. JOHN HANKIN | 224 |

# POETRY AND CONDUCT

WHEN every philosophy has been tested, when all policies have been heard and all speculations as to the destiny of man weighed one against another, it is bigotry alone that will assert that it has the last word in any argument. No social faith is ever wholly proved, there is no god but will sooner or later be dethroned, no chart of life that we can know with certainty is truly drawn. This is not unhappily so. The imagination of man is so vast an instrument, and the world of experience upon which it may work so varied and so exhilarating, that a lifetime of untiring activity will enable us at best to realise but an odd stray here and there from the thronging life that is daily waiting to be shaped to our delight. The man who is continually refusing the witness of his own imagination and is crying for the assurance of authorities other than his own alert spirit is withered in the centre, he is spiritually dead. You may be sorry for him; his misfortune may be explained. Life may have dealt so hardly with him, his nature may be so little robust or may have been so ill-tended, that he cannot oppose calamity with the resources of his own resilient character and imagination. But compassion and a recognition of causes do not alter the fact that here is spiritual death—the most lamentable, as it is, perhaps, the commonest of all tragedies. It is a tragedy that permeates society, thriving even when there is no bitter burden of cruel experience to excuse or at least to explain it. Flourishing trades are built upon it. We all know the unfortunate people whose spiritual lethargy is so profound, who are so insensible to the calls of the innumerable adventures that are in every wind and bough and footstep, that they will pay sly palmists to tell them of a to-morrow that they may be sure will be duller than to-day. It is a tragedy that our newspapers exploit with a certain knowledge of profit. So general is the apathy in which we move that a placard promising us a sensation—it is the very word of common use—will sell a paper to three men out of four as they pass.

## POETRY AND CONDUCT

This pervading dullness of spirit is the gravest penalty that we pay for an over-specialised civilisation. There are so many things that, in the state which we have blindly chosen, have to be done by routine and example, that routine and example have become habits with us, creeping from what should be their lowly station of servility and warping the free functions of our imagination. That this should be so is tragic chiefly because it is a denial of our proudest right. If absolute knowledge is beyond our attainment, as it is, a continuity of vivid experience is not beyond our attainment, and such activity of experience is the fulfilment of the highest function of which man is capable. It is health; it is peace—the peace that passeth all understanding, that is, the peace that is greater than all understanding. Its full and perfect realisation is, perhaps, impossible, but that it can be realised in some measure is the hope, indeed the certainty, that makes this perplexing and capricious life so greatly worth living. That this experience includes sorrow does not affect the question. It is the act of experiencing that matters, that exercises our nature in the only full and significant way. And out of this exercise, this alertness of our nature, which is in and for itself of supreme importance to us as individuals, comes a sure and single sense of justice, which is of equal importance to us as members of society. For all injustice, and injustice is the only social evil, or we may say that it covers all social evils, is born of spiritual lethargy. When a man's thought is alert, when his spirit is responsive to the beauty and awe of the world, he does not put his hand to the terrible evil of injustice.

For its direct value to us, then, as individuals, liberating as it does the highest force that is in us, and for its indirect influence upon our social integrity, this wealth of passionate experience is the thing that we must most desire. To destroy lethargy of spirit, to shape all our daily meditation and intercourse and the fertile activity of the natural world into sharp and intimately realised forms in our own imagination, is the aim of every rightly disciplined mind. And in the accomplishment of this aim the poet is he who of all men can give us the surest help. Without inquiring too

## POETRY AND CONDUCT

curiously whether the desire for this intensity of experience can in the beginning come from any external impulse, whether it must not at first make some unaided gesture, it is not questionable that once it has moved, however shyly, contact with fine poetry will of all things foster it into vigorous certainty and growth. For contact with fine poetry is precisely contact with most vital and personal experience conveyed to us in the most persuasive medium invented by man for habitual intercourse—pregnant and living words. Pregnant and living : for here is the secret of poetry. The use of words, in the common run of daily affairs, has become so much a matter of habit, so dependent upon the thousand small conventions by which we conduct the necessary or chosen routine of our lives, that it is devoid of any real significance. The common use of words is to convey from one man to another information, which is a thing quite distinct from experience, since we have trained ourselves to receive and impart a great deal of information daily out of mere custom and for the purpose of keeping pace with the exacting and often monstrous machinery that governs our society. If we could number the words passing to and from us in the course of a week that were really born of significant and urgent experience, we should have but a very small reckoning. And, not being born of this quick experience seeking to announce itself, the words are not pregnant and living, but dead. Most of the multitudes of words that are current among us have no true significance at all. I do not say that they are not necessary, or that it would be possible for men to bear the pressure of constant interchange of words that had real significance, but the fact is, none the less, that words as we continually use them for the common purposes of daily traffic mean, in the more exacting sense, nothing. It is only when they are used to convey experience that they become quick and stir in us not a mere acceptance that is barely a mental action at all, but an energy of experience that corresponds to the energy that is their source. And it is of the necessity that such experience finds, when it is most profound, to state itself in perfectly selected and ordered words, that poetry comes into being. The precision and light that are the characteristics of fine poetry can be

## POETRY AND CONDUCT

achieved by intense and individual experience and from no other source whatever. This is not to say that intensity and individuality of experience are in themselves enough to create poetry; the poet alone knows the diligence with which he must discipline his craftsmanship before he can serve his art worthily. But they are none the less the only sources of the material upon which he can hopefully direct his craftsmanship; it is from them alone that his words win their significance, and it is of them that his words speak to us, compelling in us an ecstasy which is exactly a response to that ecstasy of his own. And so it is that he, of all external influences, is the most potent in directing us to the realisation of what should be our deepest desire, spiritual activity.

So do we trace the association, profound and of far greater importance than is ever realised in the government of the world, between poetry and conduct. The old question as to whether poetry—or any art—should proclaim a moral can occupy none but dull and unimaginative minds. Poetry proclaims life; that is all and it is everything. Didactic poetry does not necessarily fail. It generally does so, and because it generally comes not of conviction, not of that urgent experience, but of the lethargic acceptance of this or that doctrine or moral attitude that is not the poet's own delighted discovery, and so we respond to it with no more than lethargic acceptance on our side. It is always a question of the poet's sincerity and conviction. Our experience in receiving his poetry must correspond to his experience in creating it, and it is experience alone that we demand of it. What the nature of the experience is does not matter, but the experience itself must be thrilling with life. This question was raised aptly enough at a debate recently in one of our universities, when a motion was put that " the trend of modern drama is and should be sociological and not poetic." That is to say, what is poetical is not sociological. I can only see one possible way of reasoning whereby so queer a conclusion can have been reached. Sociology, it must have been argued, is a practical science, concerned directly with the practical conditions of our daily lives. And then, it must have been said, poetry is something which is not so concerned. And a convenient popular

## POETRY AND CONDUCT

fallacy was ready to hand in support of the notion. For is not the poet a vague and ambitious visionary, creating in his fancy a pleasant world of retreat from the unfortunate difficulties of actual life? Does not poetry, therefore, bear the mark of its makers, being the fit concern only of people who are prepared to shut their eyes to the distressing phenomena which vex the routine of our busy days? Yes, yes—it is consoling enough at stray moments when the armour is off to indulge in this pleasant pilgrimage to Lotus land, leaving the fret and burden of affairs, of the great problems of evolution, behind us. They are good fellows, these poets, in their way, giving us enchanting interludes of make-believe against the sterner business of life. But, remember, we are serious men and women in our normal hours, facing this great seething perplexity with stubborn wills to master it if we can, and we want our drama to be serious in its aim too, to become the powerful pulpit that it may be, pointing us shortly to answering these many questions that beset us, or, better still, answering them for us outright. The poets—yes, on dreamy afternoons when, tired and dusty from the momentous struggles that are our daily use, we snatch an hour's well-earned idleness; even, in strictly governed measure, and if it be not too difficult, as a diversion from the more important matter of our morning papers. But in the theatre? No, not for two hours and a half when we would settle our minds to grave and more responsible things.

This is, unhappily, no fantastic manipulating of a case. This fundamental misunderstanding of the nature of poetry is common enough in the world, as, if it would but see it, Europe to-day should realise. Our governors have not taken art, which is spiritual activity with its consequent clear-sighted moral judgment, seriously, and we and our governors are paying the sorry penalty. But let us think a little more of that curious proposition. What is the purpose of sociology? Is it anything more or less than the better regulation of society, which is the relationship of man to his fellows? That is what all your sociologists are striving for, unless they are lost in a mere maze of theories. We are gregarious cattle, and we do not very well know how to behave to each other at all

## POETRY AND CONDUCT

times. Quite simply, as I have already said, we are unjust to one another. The sociologist examines the phenomena of this injustice in the abstract, tabulates the results, underlines as far as may be the points at which reform may most hopefully make its attacks, and suggests the methods by which such reforms should work. Admirable : full of fine zeal, often even of heroism. And your sociological dramatist, yet more sensitive to the grievous manifestations of this injustice, defines them yet more clearly through the agency of imagined men and women. Yet more admirable, striking as it does more directly at the heart. But, when all is said, all these people—the people whose sociological inquiry and enthusiasm take the form of a definite exposure of particular social injustice—are but telling us what we know. And here is the centre of the matter. I do not say that it is not a good thing to tell us what we know. I do not say that if you tell us often and eloquently enough you will not sometimes shame us into sudden resolutions that may bear fruit in some actual reparation, but I do say that to tell us what we know is not at all the same or so big a thing as to make us order that knowledge in our minds with a clear moral judgment. If, for example, you take your industrial sweater, and ask him over his lunch whether he thinks it good to steal another man's labour and food and life itself, he will tell you—no. He knows it is evil, but he does not mind evil. And you may demonstrate as clearly and as persuasively as you will to him in propaganda or on the stage or from the pulpit that this sweating is evil, and you will only have told him what he knew, and still he will not mind evil. You have done nothing to rouse him from the lethargy of spirit which is the cause of his insensibility to the ugliness of the evil that he does.

This lethargy comes of too close a preoccupation with facts. To be a man of affairs—and we are all in some measure men of affairs—generally means a too constant absorption in facts for any concern with what is really important, the significance of facts. Again, the newspapers, those great criterions of popular temper, flatter, sagely enough, a characteristic which is so general. They will tell us that a wretched clerk has defrauded his employers of five pounds, and that he has been sent to prison

## POETRY AND CONDUCT

for two years, knowing that the public is greedy for facts. But what are we told of the significance of these facts, of the surrounding circumstances, of the conflict of mind and the failure of character, of the hearts that must bear the punishment without having offended, of the wreckage of love, of the petty and odious tyrannies that have made trouble yet more difficult? Nothing; for we have no taste for these things, our spirits being inactive, not eager for experience. And our industrial sweater—a single practitioner in the evil of injustice of which we are none of us blameless, none of us being always and wholly free of this lethargy —living dully under this deadening pressure of facts, has not the spiritual wit to realise that the evil which he does is a terrible thing. He knows that it is evil, but he does not feel its terror. If, as I have said, you show him its terror very vividly and directly in your drama or otherwise, you may occasionally shock him into perception, but in nearly every case the shock will be merely temporary and effect no radical quickening of the spirit. And it is just such radical quickening of the spirit which is the only effective cure for injustice of all kinds, and, as we have seen, it is just this radical quickening of the spirit which is the highest function of poetry. The poet will commonly, in the intensity of his vision, see beyond the facts of our immediate concern as sociologists into the great eternal assertion of which these are but local and ever mutable negations. He will—not necessarily, but commonly—sing humanity with all its natural sorrows and exultations, without emphasising this or that particular folly which is only of particular application. And in doing this (let me here say that nothing is easier than for a man to deceive himself that he is doing this when he is doing no more than to repeat a bundle of hearsay generalities about which he has no real conviction whatever, and so to become that most troublesome and useless of all things—a pseudo-poet) the poet, whether we agree with what he has to say or not, quickens our imaginative perception. That is to say, he makes us alive. And, quite definitely, to be alive is to be moral. Injustice is the result of mental inertia; that is to say that unjust people, in so far as they are unjust, are spiritually dead people.

## POETRY AND CONDUCT

Remembering always that the chief distinction of poetry is that it enables men who are habitually responsive to its appeal to exult in the beauty and the heroic conflict of life, and that this other virtue, this conditioning of men's minds so that injustice becomes abhorrent, is but its secondary glory, this is the case for poetry as a sociological weapon and as the most wholesome of all influences upon conduct ; being the expression of the most intense spiritual activity to which man can attain, it, more than any other use of the common means of communication, words, begets spiritual activity in its hearers. And to combat the supreme evil of society, injustice, we need not be told that it is evil, which we know and yet persist in its practice, but to have our spiritual activity quickened, when we shall know that it is loathsome, and crush it.

Of the three principal elements of poetry as it leaves the poet a finished art, rhythm, diction, and the image, the one having the most immediate and widest appeal is rhythm with its emphasis, rhyme. Consequently, since the capacity for rhyme and simple rhythm is common, these are the qualities which are most frequently abused and in themselves mistaken for poetry when the finer spirit of poetry has left them untouched. Simple rhythms have been and are continually used by poets to contain the rarest poetic imagination, but in themselves they may be ordered by the most unpoetic minds to no better purpose than pointing reflections that have neither savour nor persuasion, and minds equally barren of imaginative fervour will give these jingles glad acceptance as shaping, a little more clearly than they have done for themselves, their own jaded moralities. And so it is that what passes for poetry is widely extolled as the most efficient of all guides to conduct by people who have in their hearts no tidings whatever of poetry and its functions. I have a little book which, although it belongs to an earlier generation, would, I am sure, find a large public to-day if its Victorian dress were re-modelled to our later modes. It is called *Learning to Converse,* and it has two splendidly instructive chapters on poetry. An impeccable uncle is teaching his nephew, Edmund, the art of polite conversation, and in a lucky thirteenth chapter he begins thus :

# POETRY AND CONDUCT

"I have not yet, Edmund, in teaching you to converse, said anything about poetry; and yet when introduced with judgment into conversation, a verse of poetry is oftentimes very effective. In prose, thoughts are frequently too much spread, while in poetry they are brought more to a point, and affect us more."

**Any doubt as to whether this childlike opening may not after all have in it the roots of wisdom is answered when a moment later Edmund is further enlightened by examples :**

"There is that in a rhyme that catches the attention and clings to the memory. Were I to say, ' Edmund, we must make hay while the sun shines—

  Now's the time, and now's the hour,
  By and by the sky may lour '—

you would see at once that the thing we had in hand was not to be neglected. And if I wanted to cheer your spirits on a dull day, hardly could I do it better than in crying out in a cheerful tone of voice—

 ' Never despair when the fog's in the air ;
  A sunshiny morning will come without warning.' "

"Oh," says Edmund with a very natural gaiety, "I should be in spirits directly."

"Again," (continues his uncle under this deplorable encouragement,) "you would be likely enough to be impressed with the uncertainty of life were one to say to you in conversation—

  Whatever paths our feet may tread,
  Our life is but a spider's thread,"

and his sagacity is confirmed by Edmund's delighted : " I think I should ; and hardly could I forget the words." But the old gentleman's appetite grows by what it feeds on, and before long he reaches triumphant heights.

" You must remember," he says, " that the effect of poetry in conversation depends much on the judgment with which it is introduced. Sometimes it is necessary to give a reproof at the moment, and there are instances of this being done with much point and discretion. It is said that Dr. Byrom once reproved an officer for swearing, in the following words—

Soldier, so tender of thy prince's fame,
Why make so free with a superior name ?
For thy king's sake the brunt of battle bear,
But, for the King of kings' sake, never swear."

" He would not be likely to forget them. They are very striking," says Edmund with commendable insight, and so the incorrigible old man goes his iniquitous way.

It all sounds very queer, doubtless. The trick of speech has changed. There is to-day nothing ingenious in the heavy Victorian formality to conceal the emasculation of mind and the absurdity of it all, which are patent enough as we read this little volume of misbegotten humour. As it is set

## POETRY AND CONDUCT

down here the most guileless uncle of to-day would see that there was something amiss in the manner of instruction, and the most unsophisticated Edmund would be suspicious. But the sentiment has lost none of its power. We can very well imagine a popular novelist of to-day saying a good word for an equally popular rhymester something in this way :

The Duke put his hand on the boy's shoulder. Having no son of his own, his nephew was dearer to him than anything in the world, and he never tired in his affectionate admonitions. " Stick to your games, my boy," he would often say, " and always play the game. You must be a manly man. But don't be ashamed of your books. I read a little poetry myself, and often repeat the lines—
>   Laugh, and the world laughs with you,
>     Weep, and you weep alone,
>   For this sad old earth must borrow its mirth,
>     But has sorrow enough of its own."

The boy's mind was already susceptible enough to respond vaguely to the beauty of sentiment in the poet's lines, of which his uncle kept a goodly store in his memory.

It need hardly be said that verse such as " Laugh, and the world laughs with you," which makes its appeal by confirming, with an easy trick of rhythm and rhyme, the trite moral reflections with which the minds of its admirers are already well stocked, has no reference to or influence upon the spiritual activity of man. It is not, in any full sense, poetry. It has rhythm, but it has neither excellence of diction nor imaginative intensity. That is to say, the rhythmic impulse is used not to accentuate the imaging of some urgently perceived mood or idea in superbly chosen and ordered words, but merely to gratify a very common habit of mind, the unctuous parading of easy platitudes, by associating it with an equally common instinct—one which when expressed passes generally enough for poetry, but is in itself no more poetry than is a dictionary. Again, I will not say that those lines about " the sad old earth " have never been of any benefit to anybody. They may have been, just as, I suppose, somebody or another may have been saved from indiscretion by remembering that you should look before you leap, or that you cannot eat your cake and have it. These proverbial sayings, indeed, have a certain flavour if we can distinguish it from the thick dust of constant usage, but they do not work in the way which is poetry's, and still less do the devices of the didactic rhymester. They may sometimes regulate a man's discretion, but they

## POETRY AND CONDUCT

can never penetrate to the roots of his spiritual being, quickening it with the provocative power that is art's alone. Born of and communicating urgent life ; that is the nature of poetry, and it is mere futility to confuse it with the facile rhyming that comes from borrowed and half-realised emotion and impresses nothing but a dull inertia of acceptance. It matters not at all whether the poet's utterance controls an emotion that has no apparent strain of moral contemplation, as in :

> In Xanadu did Kubla Khan
>   A stately pleasure dome decree :
> Where Alph, the sacred river, ran
> Through caverns measureless to man
>   Down to a sunless sea,

or one that has so direct and obvious a significance as :

> To-morrow, and to-morrow, and to-morrow,
> Creeps in this petty pace from day to day,
> To the last syllable of recorded time ;
> And all our yesterdays have lighted fools
> The way to dusty death. Out, out, brief candle !
> Life's but a walking shadow, a poor player
> That struts and frets his hour upon the stage,
> And then is heard no more ; it is a tale
> Told by an idiot, full of sound and fury,
> Signifying nothing.

In either case we are aware, unless we are fundamentally insensible to the challenge of poetry, of a strange and lovely imaginative ardour within us, responding eagerly to the energy from which the poet's word has sprung. And of such ardour, and of such alone, comes all sanity.

There have not been wanting voices to proclaim that in these terrible days such things as poetry have no proper place. It is new witness of the profound misunderstanding of art that is almost desperately prevalent. Never was the world so deeply, so critically in need of the persuasive influence of poetry as it is to-day. I am not here concerned with the poetry that has actually been produced by the war. There has already been some fine work done, more, perhaps, than might have been expected, and there has been a great deal of work done that is wholly negligible for any positive qualities, but curiously interesting as a sign of the times. The gigantic shock that has fallen upon Europe has startled great numbers of people from the lethargy of thought and feeling of which I have spoken. The immediate results have been rather unpleasant than gracious. The people

## POETRY AND CONDUCT

who, before August, 1914, in normal times and under relatively simple conditions, had not one thought in their heads to rub against another, have suddenly been confronted by a situation about which they cannot escape from having some ideas, and with irresponsible arrogance they now assume, in conditions that are extraordinarily complex and difficult for every thinking mind, the right to direct and censure the conduct of their neighbours with the most impudent assurance. And so with the people, equally numerous, who before this catastrophe had no very defined feeling about anything. They, too, have suddenly been forced against a circumstance that makes complete absence of emotion no longer possible. And a great many of them have, unfortunately, hurried to relieve the emotion by translating it into verse without having any poetic equipment. There is not really in them a sudden access of full emotional life ; that is not a thing that waits for its being upon some violence of event. They have merely passed from lethargy to vague excitement, which is the habitual state of the ineffective rhymester. But, troublesome as are the first manifestations of this new activity, the activity is there. To think arrogantly is better than not to think at all, and to be excited is better than to be lethargic. It may safely be said that never in history has there been so vast a force of incipient spiritual activity to be influenced for good or evil as there is to-day, and it is the duty of every artist and every man and woman who cares for art and understands its meaning to labour at this moment with the most loyal determination to foster and establish the power which, springing from alert and supple and just activity in the spirits of its creators, would, if duly heeded, more surely than any other bring this stirring of the seed to a prosperous harvest.

# THE VALUE OF POETRY IN EDUCATION

THE gravest indictment of our educational systems is that they callously and persistently neglect art. They seek continually to store our minds with information, information that is often desirable and excellent, without seeking to quicken our receptive faculty. They sow broadly, but they do not prepare the ground. With reckless and disastrous waste of power they cast, upon the barren places of our mere acceptance, statements, doctrines, counsels, that can fertilise only in the soil of experience. Since language is our habitual means of communication, I propose, in considering how this misdirection of energy might be corrected by art, to speak only of the highest verbal art, poetry, though the same reasoning might in substance be applied to the use of music, painting, and all arts alike. The poet, then, in his work, no less than the pedagogue, presents some statement, doctrine or counsel. He sees or believes something that his impulse to poetry bids him to mould into the form which is art. But he does more than this; he not only sees or believes, he also states his vision or belief in such a way that we cannot fail to respond to his experience with a real experience of our own, and the essential value of his poetry to us lies not in the vision or belief that is stated, but in our response to the statement. It may be that his vision is one that is outside the habit of our own thought, or that his belief is one to which we do not assent, but that is no matter. There is a precious enrichment of our nature in the very act of perceiving, despite all disagreement. And it is such enrichment of our nature that above all else enables us to take our share fitly in the government of the world.

It would be a mistake to suggest that to make us ripe for this government is the highest function of the enrichment of which I speak. That would be to flatter the far too common fallacy of setting the State above the individual. A fine appreciation of poetry brings to the individual a spiritual ecstasy

## VALUE OF POETRY IN EDUCATION

that transcends all morality, but the capacity for such appreciation also fosters a justness in moral judgment that is the most desirable end of formal education and yet the one that it most commonly fails to achieve. We need not here open the difficult question as to whether the poet—or the creative artist generally—is, in the exercise of his gift, likely to make for more or less moral excellence in himself. The creative artists must always be few, and their personal morality one way or the other cannot affect the morality of the State more noticeably than can that of any other handful of men. In some cases there may be no surplus for anything else when the energy necessary to creation has been consumed, in others it may be plentiful; that is all, and the question is not to the present purpose. But that a living responsiveness to the challenge of poetry is almost inevitably coincident with moral health is beyond all doubt, and, I think, for a reason that is easily defined.

Cardinal morality is the system evolved by long generations of men as being the wisest and cleanest for governing their intercourse. The thousand conventions and institutions that decline so freely from conveniences to superstitions have nothing to do with morality. It is neither moral nor immoral to drink gin or to have three wives. These are not questions of morality ; in the one case it is simply a question of how much you drink, in the other of where you live. But uncharitableness, greed, tyranny, lust for power over any but ourselves, bearing false witness, reluctance to see others fortunate—such things as these are immoralities always and everywhere. And they are immoralities that the essential nature of man, if only it be allowed to realise itself, denounces and attacks. If only it be allowed to realise itself. There is the whole difficulty, in the easing of which lies the paramount duty of education.

Merely to tell a child that to deprive another of his dues is wrong, or that " Might is right " is a dishonourable ethic, or that intemperance of all kinds is a savage cruelty, is to beat wings in a vacuum. Assertion of this sort can never take flight. The child either knows these things already, or he will not understand you. If he knows them already it is by the exercise of his instinctive morality working out from the first realisation of

## VALUE OF POETRY IN EDUCATION

his essential nature. If he does not know them, it is futile to tell him. The real service that is in our power is to help him towards that realisation, and so towards his own moral discovery of the things that we have vainly asserted. There is no surer way of doing this than to encourage him in the contemplation of significant and imaginative speech ; and the most significant and imaginative speech is poetry.

In bringing poetry to the service of education, there are two subtle dangers to which we must be very sensitive. The first is the danger of choosing for our purpose poetry not for its power of signifying, but for the particular thing that it signifies ; to choose, say :

> Be good, sweet maid, and let who can be clever ;
>   Do lovely things, not dream them all day long ;
> And so make Life, and Death, and that For Ever
>   One grand sweet song,

rather than :

>   It ceased ; yet still the sails made on
>   A pleasant noise till noon,
>   A noise like of a hidden brook
>   In the leafy month of June,
>   That to the sleeping woods all night
>   Singeth a quiet tune,

because of Kingsley's explicit charge to virtue. We must remember that explicit charges to virtue are no longer our concern, and we are now seeking something that will best quicken the power of responsiveness in the pupil. There is little or no life in Kingsley's words, and they leave us inert ; but Coleridge's are quick, beating out in a million waves, and we become all eagerness as we hear them, and under that eagerness stirs refreshed the faculty of moral justness :

> A noise like of a hidden brook
> In the leafy month of June,
> That to the sleeping woods all night
> Singeth a quiet tune.

The second danger, which is really a refinement of the first, is that of lazily deceiving ourselves as to what is significant language. If our imagination is sluggish, the second-rate or even the spurious will easily impose upon us. In nothing do we blunder more readily than in the belief that we are being impressed when we are not—an idle frailty that accounts in most cases for the extraordinary importance that is given to the leader-writers in

## VALUE OF POETRY IN EDUCATION

our newspapers. An adroit use of language that is so familiar as to be meaningless will, unless we are very vigilant, tempt us into the belief that we are agog with responsiveness, while we are in truth doing no more than purr in our sleep. For instance:

>   Nothing remains but the Eternal Nameless
>       And all-creative spirit of the Law,
>   Uncomprehended, comprehensive, blameless,
>       Invincible, resistless, with no flaw ;
>   So full of love it must create forever,
>       Destroying that it may create again—
>   Persisting and perfecting in endeavour,
>       It yet must bring forth angels, after men—
>           This, this remains.

Here is an opinion which has an air of gravity, and it is set out in sounding fashion. But what do these lines really mean? What is their significance? Nothing. We sleep on, purring or not as the case may be. Many people have purred loudly as they read those lines no doubt—they are by an admired American poetess—believing themselves to be quivering with vital perceptions. But we have only to recall some other rhyme, telling of things as plain and simple as you will, but telling of them in language really significant, to realise the difference even if we cannot explain it :

> Fear no more the heat o' the sun,
>   Nor the furious winter's rages ;
> Thou thy worldly task hast done,
>   Home art gone and ta'en thy wages :
> Golden lads and girls all must,
> As chimney-sweepers, come to dust.

When you have taught a child to know the value of that

> As chimney-sweepers, come to dust,

you have done more for his moral sense than will ever be done by the whole maze of text-book information and precept. If we had an educational system that accustomed the child's intelligence to habitual contact with the humane and resilient beauty of such words as these, we should be laying the foundations of a truer citizenship than the modern world has known.

This is not an occasion upon which to discuss the difficulties and practical means of organising the new education that shall take poetry for its strongest instrument. To find teachers whose own judgment is delicate and balanced in the

## VALUE OF POETRY IN EDUCATION

choice of the material to be used, and who can then decide how to use it to the best advantage, will not be easy to do, but it will be possible. And I believe it to be, almost more than anything else in our social effort, worth doing. Modern civilisation has looked upon art as a luxury, a delight for idle moments, the dreams of a few unpractical visionaries, and modern civilisation has failed, and I will add that it has failed directly in consequence of this neglect of art. Our housing reforms, our Insurance Acts, our old-age pensions, our minimum wage bills, our factory legislation—all these things are but a patching of the pot at one place while it is beginning to leak at another. Government is but education grown up, and in both modern civilisation has made the same mistake. We tell people that they must seek beauty, and we take no steps to enable them to recognise it. We tinker with the surface of their lives and leave the central source untouched. For example, a great deal has been said about the state of our rural populations. Much effort has been spent on the mending of their housing and general economic conditions. We tell a man that he should have a decent house ; we even pay to have his house made decent. But it is a waste of energy, because he does not understand. To take this one question alone, here is a way in which the authorities may effect a fundamental rural reform. Let them use some of the money available for the purpose to send companies into the villages to play Shakespeare, and the work of other great or fine dramatists, and in less than a generation the people will desire decent conditions, and as soon as they desire them they will have them. This is no fantastic plea. It is time that we who care for art and understand its character insisted roundly and in every season that we are the strictly practical people, that we are the people who have our eyes set straight, not squinting, and so can see beyond our noses. And the supreme hope of the world is that in nearly every one of us lies the capacity for this understanding of art. Our education hitherto has contentedly gone its way, asserting, asserting, asserting; we come out of it with our consciousness latent and dulled, and as a result we go through life accepting the catch-cries of expedience or so-called interest instead of

## VALUE OF POETRY IN EDUCATION

framing a clear moral judgment. The faculty in us which might so frame has never been stirred. But all this would have been changed if from the dawning of our intelligence we had been called into activity by the alert and provocative spirit of poetry. We must demand our rights in this matter. Here is the new crusade. Civilisation has had generations in which to prove a system of education and government that disregards the power of art. And the result? Our social evils fester year after year, and our system does no more than cover them fearfully up, while our national morality—I am speaking of modern civilisation as a whole—bears fruit in the hideous and blasphemous tragedy that has fallen upon Europe to-day. Our hand in this immediate circumstance has been honourable, but has nevertheless been forced to the sword, but you will not find a man in Europe whose moral judgment has been evolved in that spiritual activity that is induced by habitual responsiveness to noble poetry who would have lent his sanction to the policies in which all the nations have carried themselves to this unthinkable madness. No: the method chosen by civilisation to conduct its social affairs has failed lamentably and disastrously, and again I say that it has failed because it has refused to accept the immeasurable services of art in quickening the nature of man so that he may develop his native morality to its full efficiency. I do not suggest, I need hardly say, that familiarity with art is the only way in which man's consciousness may attain the activity that releases his highest moral sense, but I do say that it is incomparably the surest and most efficient way. And it is the way that we should insist, with every authority that we can control or influence, should now be attempted. When we have passed through this present calamity, social reorganisation will inevitably begin on a scale hitherto unknown. And we must get down to the roots. We must turn from the enunciation of moral principles to the fostering of man's spiritual activity. If we can contrive this, moral principles may safely be left to assert themselves with justice and sanity. And in the education of the spirit poetry is an invincible ally, ready to our hand. If for one decade our children

## VALUE OF POETRY IN EDUCATION

could be intelligently guided into frequent contact with the life that informs all great poetry, the vast majority of them would respond to that life, and out of the response would spring the regeneration of mankind.

# THE POET AND HIS VISION

A PASSION for poetry must spring, it would seem, from one of two desires. Either we seek to enlarge our experience, or we seek to establish it by external and independent testimony. The former desire makes for catholicity and eager adventurousness, the latter for selection and rejection. The profoundest lesson that man has learnt in his brief history is that he must not hope for any perfect revelation of fixed and central truth, that, indeed, abstract truth is as fabulous a rumour as the philosopher's stone. We no longer hope for a happy chance that shall guide our hand to the hidden corner of the world's veil, and, enabling us to draw it aside, leave the riddle solved for ever. As to the source and destiny of this, our present life, men are forced, for all their hundred hopes and dreams, into an heroic stoicism or an heroic faith ; but, rightly considered, this life itself is not a problem at all, but a vision. Not an abstract

## THE POET AND HIS VISION

vision that we may by the grace of God come up to one of these fine days, but a definite vision created anew by every temperament. It is to state the fact too curiously to say that the external world has no existence outside our own consciousness, but every vision is wrought of this element, unchanging and self-existent it may be, and a consciousness that is distinct from all others. There is a common factor in the terror of James Thomson and the heroic courage of William Morris. The City of Dreadful Night and the windy places of Hindfell are of the same world, but they are wrought through conflicting temperaments into wholly divergent visions. Both revelations are infinitely remote from the phantom of abstract truth, yet both are eternally true with the truth of existence itself. Whether or no we are concerned in both depends upon our mental disposition. If we desire to explore the experiences of all men, then we shall approach both, not to confirm our own intuitions, but with minds gladly receptive. If we feel that the only safety in life lies in strengthening against all weather our chosen philosophic and spiritual moorings, then we shall mistrust the vision that does not coincide in some measure with our own. There is no doubt as to which course makes for riper charity among men, but it is equally certain that to some a sacrifice of such charity is necessary for their peace.

It is this factor of temperament in vision, as apart from the thing seen, that makes the classification of poets in terms of an epoch so dangerous. It is no very helpful system that couples the names of Webster and Spenser, Milton and Suckling, Blake and Gray, Wordsworth and Keats, Tennyson and Browning, Morris and Swinburne. It may be true to say that in every age there are peculiar manifestations in the general life of mankind which combine with the eternal things of nature and humanity to make up the thing seen, and that they also will combine in each case with the poet's temperament to create the vision, resulting in some small degree in a common factor in the work of the poets of an age. But beyond this it is not safe to go. It may happen at times by accident that a group of poets, working together in close intimacy or under some powerful common influence, will produce work of a like texture, but it

## THE POET AND HIS VISION

is by accident only, and it is a consideration that never applies to poets of the first rank. Ben Jonson, the greatest of the many great men whom we do nothing to deserve, uttered one of the most superbly right critical phrases in literature when he said that his friend was not for an age but for all time. His word has become diluted to an echo by much repetition ; but, freshly read, it contains the seed of all critical wisdom in this matter. It is almost a negligible part of the poet's function to reflect his age. The poet is to hold the mirror up to Nature, and the mirror is his own temperament. How will the world look seen through that ? This, at any rate for those of us who dare embark upon the adventure at all, careless for the moment of the reflection in our own particular mirror, is our sole curiosity.

When Swinburne's *Poems and Ballads* appeared it created a profound impression, which at least was something for a book of poems to do with an unknown name on the title-page. The sensation, however, was not one of delight in the discovery of a great new poet, but one of shock to the manners of the time. The phase of Victorianism that expressed itself in pious respectability was rudely upset by this exultant voluptuary in song, and in consequence his voluptuousness itself is commonly set down as the product of revolt, as something deliberately designed to clear the air of immoral righteousness. It was, of course, nothing of the sort, but the finely unbridled expression of the poet's temperament. It is highly improbable that Swinburne, when he was writing his first poems, or at any time save when he was making a direct challenge, gave a thought to the intellectual philistinism that he did so much to kill. It is vain to deny or to assert that the obscure power that controls the Universe sent this wholesomely corrective influence at the precisely appropriate moment, but in any case the influence itself was certainly unconscious of this particular aspect of its function, save in so far as the evil thing was an element in the great composite world that was reflected in the poet's temperament and wrought into the durable record of vision in these poems. To look upon *Poems and Ballads* as chiefly, or even considerably, important by virtue of their destructive and revolutionary qualities is wholly to

## THE POET AND HIS VISION

misunderstand the nature of poetry. To think of them in this way is to deny them all hope of permanence, for it makes their achievement one that is necessarily forgotten with the encompassing of their purpose. It is to make anew the mistake of praising art for its destructive, rather than its creative, qualities. That manifestation of his age was, in the cosmos that Swinburne contemplated, no more than a speck of dust on the great shining pattern of life; he brushed it aside, but to suppose that it troubled him seriously or claimed more than momentary attention is to think in ill proportions.

The fact is that we are in danger of becoming the slaves of a fallacy. We have been told that the best study of history is to be found in the literature of the ages. But it is necessary to choose the literature, and that not the highest creative literature. Can it be advanced as a serious proposition that it would be possible to reconstruct, even vaguely, Greek civilisation and custom from Sophocles and Euripides, or Elizabethan England from Shakespeare, or the Commonwealth from Milton, or any age at all from Blake, or Shelley, or Morris? Of course not. There are certain indications of current standards implied in the work of these men, indications made more profoundly by them than by lesser writers; but the only thing as to which we can pronounce with any certainty is the temperament through which they saw the eternal things. And this is, moreover, the only thing about which a passion for poetry will make us curious, whatever kind of curiosity we may have for other reasons. It is true to say that the Puritan Age helped to make Milton, and that it was in some measure responsible for the moulding of his temperament; but this does not affect the fact that our interest is in what Milton thought of the world as Milton, however he may have been fashioned, and not in what he may be able to tell us of the spiritual and intellectual opinions of Puritans in the aggregate. We honour our poets, and turn to them, not because they are like the rest of men, but because they are gloriously unlike. History, at best, is but a very vague approximation. To know the history of the world would be to see clearly into the myriad temperaments into which the world has been reflected, each making its own separate image. Now and again it is given

## THE POET AND HIS VISION

to one in the millions to leave some record of his vision, and that man is the poet. Through this circumstance we are given the priceless privilege of unrestricted intimacy with another mind, and that, if we could but realise it, is the holiest gift that is to man. А poet can no more be the concentrated expression of an age than a mayor can of a city, and we wrong both ourselves and him if we neglect the distinction of his separate entity in seeking a kind of composite abstraction.

The nature of the poet's vision is not to be confused with his technical equipment. It is questionable whether the acutest critic could assign, say, our twelve greatest poets to their proper epochs from internal evidence. If he were able to do so, it would be from the evidence of technique, in which some sort of historical growth and development can be traced, and from stray references to inessential things. It certainly would not be from those things of the poet's vision that were most lofty and memorable, not from the essential revelation of his temperament. A poet might have had Browning's vision in the seventeenth century, or Milton's in the nineteenth. To realise this is to realise that poetry is a thing of fundamental and eternal values, and that the vitality of its continuous manifestation through the centuries depends, not upon the slow evolution of humanity in the mass, but upon the inexhaustible caprice that bestows upon every man a strangely new temperament. The poet's business is not to express his age, but to express himself; not to reveal truth, but to reveal himself. This is not to exalt a dreamy subjectivity; to express himself fully, he must show us how the external world appears to him. But it is time that we left off talking of an age as though it were a realisable unit, instead of being, as it really is, a medley of conflicting and largely unrelated individualities, and of truth as though it were a pearl, and the only trouble was to find the right oyster. Abstractions and generalities are useful, even necessary, in the practical working of the State and institutions; but poetry has nothing to do with them; and nothing is more dangerous to our intellectual balance than to magnify their real importance. It leads us, for example, into the error of thinking that Parliament governs the country, whilst the

## THE POET AND HIS VISION

essential things of our lives are as uncontrolled by Parliament as are the stars. The supreme distinction of poetry is that it is an eternal testimony to the richest birthright of us all, a separate personality, and the power to blend it with the external world into a new vision. Poetry is the record of the few who are able to find for the vision permanent expression.

It is possible for criticism to be quite logical, and yet, at the same time, quite insincere. It may be shown conclusively, for example, that Swinburne did actually destroy much that was unworthy in the days that immediately preceded him; but if we make this the chief reason of our praise, we are praising a thing that we do not very greatly value. Victorian prudery is nothing to us to-day, and we are not really deeply moved by the spectacle of its destruction. Emotionally, we treasure Swinburne's poetry because it tells us, in the highest manner of utterance of which man is capable, how one of our fellows saw the natural beauty of the world, and love, and the charities and pity of humanity, what figure the universe threw in the mirror that was his mind.

# ART AND THE ARTIST

WHETHER the appetite for crumbs from the table of the elect is more prevalent to-day than in the past may reasonably be questioned. Doubtless the small folk who revolved round the gallants of the Elizabethan theatre, and at a later date round the wits of the coffee-houses, were not less eager than their posterity of to-day to carry away scraps of gossip and tokens of intimacy from the distinguished company in which they foregathered. The passion for traffic in inessentials is not new, but it has been reserved for our own time to foster it into its most malevolent phase. Hitherto its operation has been confined to the few who by circumstance could come into direct contact with eminence; to-day it is a most acute menace to all the finer things of art. It has made vigorous an affectation of culture which merely bewilders the uninitiated and disgusts the humble and wise.

## ART AND THE ARTIST

The number of books published every year devoted neither to sincere criticism nor sincere biography, but frankly to chatter and nonsense concerning the great, is lamentable. For the makers of these sham chronicles to flatter themselves that the influence of their work is at worst a negative one, is foolish if not dishonest. It is harmful in a peculiarly subtle and vicious way.

The Puritan Revolution in England had for its foundation a zeal of singular purity, and it was prosecuted with an energy that has had, perhaps, no parallel in the world's history in the loftiness and singleness of its aim. But by a combination of circumstances which cannot even be outlined here, it made it momentarily impossible for the English temper rightly to understand art, and from this sudden darkening of the æsthetic vision we have not yet, as a nation, fully recovered. The motives that induced this intolerance in the poorer yet potent spirits of the revolution are perfectly intelligible, if not excusable. The mistrust of beauty was, perhaps, the heaviest price that we had to pay for an intellectual freedom that was new in the records of the nations, but lamentable as the damage was, it was not irreparable. Once in our history we have understood that art is essential to national sanity and well-being; the Elizabethan had a full and clear sense of beauty. This sense was stifled by men who, having other work to their hands, destroyed much good together with intolerable evil. It was for their children to re-create, or rather to re-invigorate, a faculty which of all others most clearly gives man his sovereignty. Slowly the instinct for the fit did its work, and we have to-day made some recovery of our lost heritage. Art is still distrusted, but it is no longer outlawed, and we are beginning once again to realise as a people that life which is not exultant and unashamed in its perception of beauty and the excellence of naked truth, is life incomplete and full of mean suspicions. And now, at a time when this new harvest most needs care and thoughtful fostering, it is threatened by a danger that is no mere scarecrow.

A wise and deep understanding of character is one of the rarest as it is one of the most precious of man's possessions. The common standards are those of custom and expediency, and however much we may deplore the fact it is folly not to recognise it. Nicely to adjust circumstance with causes and appearances with fact is reserved for the few. The popular mind is concerned only to see how circumstance and appearance shape to its own familiar pattern, and its judgment depends on this alone. That a right relation to art itself is the only discipline that can develop this criticism from dullness to distinction need not be urged here. The point vital to this present consideration is that whatever truth there may be—and finally there is much—in the assertion that the man of genius must be measured by an uncommon standard as to that superficiality of character which we misname morality, the truth is one which the popular mind cannot possibly accept, and until the popular mind has developed and strengthened itself, it is an error gravely culpable to force upon it facts which it must inevitably misinterpret.

At the present moment the chief topics of conversation among the people who are nurtured on what has been appropriately called " culturine " are Wagner and Shelley : rather, grotesque lights thrown from obscure facets of Wagner and Shelley. In Wagner's case he is, in some small measure, himself to blame. His autobiography has, of course, been carefully misrepresented by means of liberal extracts set out by critics who know their public, but the fact remains that it leaves the impression of a man who can by no deftness be made to fit into the pattern. Chatter about Shelley is becoming a cult ; volumes of it have come from the press within the past few years ; doubtless more volumes are to follow. And in Shelley's case the result is the same : we are left with a character hopelessly at variance with the pattern. The reason is, of course, perfectly obvious. Wagner's autobiography and chatter about Shelley give us only the quaint and scandalous incidents of character which are mere monstrosities until they are assigned to their proper place in the complete figure, which is to be seen alone through Wagner's music and Shelley's poetry, and in no other way whatsoever. But the popular mind cannot understand this, and it treasures up for itself the memory of a Wagner

## ART AND THE ARTIST

who was disloyal to his friends, and insolent to his benefactors, and a Shelley who had hallucinations and was an irresponsible apostle of free-love. To the people who know the music and the poetry these things are harmless ; the knowledge itself implies a faculty of rejection and interpretation that insure safety. But these people are a small minority—a minority unhappily ignorant of the temper of the majority, almost of the majority's existence. And to this majority incalculable harm is done by the chatter and caricature. A certain section, of course, delights in it all merely on account of the scandal and interrupted privacy, but a far greater section to whom the false rumours filter through is sincerely disturbed and offended. That it should be so is pitiable, but that it is so is unquestionable. And the misunderstanding and prejudice which are so generated are by no means the least considerable obstacles in the way of the re-vitalising of art as a national influence. The old resentment and mistrust of beauty are stirred up again by the discrediting of the men who have created beauty. The black side of the Puritan temper has not yet been turned wholly to the light, and in these false reports—false because shamefully incomplete—it finds for its own contentment the fullest vindication of its sinister moroseness.

Sincere and acute criticism and broadly conceived biographical statement are, of course, of immense value. They help to make our understanding of the artist's work—which should be our single purpose—more profitable and complete ; they disentangle difficulties and resolve obscurities. To the critic and to the biographer we owe honour and gratitude, and we are not grudging in our payment. Knowing that it is not given them to create, they are yet eager to do some service, and they become honourable interpreters. But the scavengers, who write for no reason save that by doing so they gain a few pence and a little notoriety, are pests. And they are at this time dangerous pests. In these things the supply creates the demand. It is so in art, and it is so in the prostitution of art. Through the energy and enthusiasm of a few just men, beauty is being set up once again in the market-place, and the people are gathering round to see and be refreshed. It is a time full of difficulty and doubt, but of

## ART AND THE ARTIST

tremendous possibilities. No danger must be unwatched, and here we have one, deadly though tricked out in bright colours and seductive in its bearing, and it needs to be crushed.

## CHAUCER: THE POET OF SPRING

By a gracious whim of circumstance, the earliest English poet of the first order, Geoffrey Chaucer, had in his blood nothing austere or sombre; his song was the spring-note of our verse, and into it he freely wove spring only of all the moods of nature. A light-hearted, gracious-humoured man, the blown rose and withered leaf had no place in his poetry. His constant charity of temper at no time allowed him to look upon the tragic follies of human affairs for more than a brief moment. When the conduct of his story leads him to the contemplation of sorrow or ruined frailty, he makes a simple statement of the happening and passes from it without elaboration. But when he is singing, as he usually is, of laughter and good luck, he waits on them delightedly, and then it is that he turns continually to nature for colours

## CHAUCER: THE POET OF SPRING

whereby to heighten his expression and bear witness to his exultation in the beauty of health and the sanctity of joy. His attitude towards nature, as expressed in his poetry, is wholly objective; he sees the spring flowers and hears the song of the birds, and they make him glad. He never suggests for a moment that nature is in any way related to his own personality, or that she is rejoicing with him. His only concern is that her sweetness and happiness are infectious, and that a virtue is constantly passing out of her for him to gather who will. The benefaction is unconscious on her part, a gracious dispensation of God.

> For certes, as at my devys,
> There is no place in paradys
> So good in for to dwelle or be
> As in that Gardin, thoughte me;
> For there was many a brid singing,
> Throughoute the yerde al thringing.
> In many places where nightingales,
> Alpes, finches, and wodewales,
> That in her swete song delyten,
> In thilke place as they habyten. . . .
>
> . . . . .
>
> And, trusteth wel, whan I hem hearde,
> Full lustily and wel I ferde;
>
> . . . . .

## PROSE PAPERS

> And certes, when I herde hir song,
> And saw the grene place among,
> In herte I wex so wonder gay,
> That I was never erst, er that day,
> So jolyf, nor so wel bigo,
> Ne mery in herte, as I was tho.

So fine a faculty is, indeed, not fashioned piecemeal; perception that rejoices in the hawthorn and the tender colours of spring is not unstirred by the golden sheaves and the barren majesty of winter. But these emblems of change and the passing of beauty were of no service to Chaucer as poet; nature as a theme in his song he never accepted, but she was an inexhaustible symbol when he meditated the sweeter humours of the world. April has never since possessed any poet's blood quite so fully. A bird in spring song was enough at any moment to fill all earth with laughter for him. The sound will send him into the very garrulousness of delight.

> The bridges that han left hir song,
> Whyl they han suffred cold so strong
> In wedres grille, and derk to sighte,
> Ben in May, for the sonne brighte,
> So glade, that they shewe in singing,
> That in hir herte is swich lyking,

# CHAUCER: THE POET OF SPRING

> That they mote singen an be light.
> Than doth the nightingale hir might
> To maken noyse, an singen blythe;
> Than is blissful, many a sythe,
> The chelaundre and the papinjay.
> Than yonge folk entenden ay
> For to ben gay and amorous,
> The time is than so savorous.

Everywhere, from *The Romaunt* to *The Canterbury Tales*, it is the same. When Sir Mirthe comes into the garden it is
to here
> The briddes, how they singen clere,
> The mavis and the nightingale,
> And other joly briddes smale,

and of the Lady Beauty he tells us

> Hir flesh was tendre as dewe of flour,
> Hir chere was simple as byrde in bour.

In *The Book of the Duchess* he cannot bear that even the sorrowful lament of the bereaved lover should be set in gloom. The poet dreams that he hears the sound of

> Men, hors, houndes, and other thing,

and joining the hunt he meets the forlorn man who unburdens himself of his sorrow at length. But he

# PROSE PAPERS

is careful to tell us that before this, as his dream opens, he thought that it was May, and that he

> was waked
> With smale foules a gret hepe,
> That had affrayed me out of slepe
> Through noyse and swetnesse of hir song;
> And, as me mette, they sate among,
> Upon my chambre-roof withoute,
> Upon the tyles, al a-boute,
> And songen—

and then :

> through the glas the sunne shon
> Upon my bed with brighte bemes,
> With many glade gilden stremes;
> And eek the welken was so fair,
> Blew, bright, clere was the air,
> And ful atempre, for sothe, hit was;
> For nother cold nor hoot hit nas.
> Ne in al the welken was a cloude.

In his greatest poem Chaucer makes but little use of natural illustration. The famous opening

> Whan that Aprille with his shoures sote
> The droghte of Marche hath perced to the rote,
> And bathed every veyne in swich licour,
> Of which vertue engendred is the flour;
> . . . . .
> Than longen folk to groon on pilgrimages,

## CHAUCER: THE POET OF SPRING

is followed up by no reflections on the changes of the days as the pilgrims travel nor on the country through which they pass. At rare intervals only in the course of the tales do we find the poet's old eagerness to point some beauty of mind or body by nature's greenness, as in the lovely line in the Knight's tale, where we are told that Emelye

> fairer was to sene
> Than is the lilie upon his stalke green.

In the same tale, just before the fateful meeting between Arcite and Palamoun in the grove, we find Chaucer again characteristically mellowing the coming trouble by setting the event in the sweet May dawn:

> The bisy larke, messager of day,
> Saluëth in hir song the morwe gray;
> And fyry Phebus ryseth up so brighte,
> That al the orient laugheth of the lighte,
> And with his stremes dryeth in the greves
> The silver dropes hanging on the leves.

Once, in the Miller's tale, he turns to autumn for a simile when he says of the carpenter's wife that

> Her mouth was swete as bragot or the meeth
> Or hord of apples leyed in hey or heeth,

and, again, there is a reminiscence of the full year in the Squire's tale :

> The vapour, which that fro the erthe glood,
> Made the sonne to seme rody and brood.

These, however, are isolated instances. Still rarer are the occasions upon which he draws any moral from nature. Once or twice only in all his poetry do we come to such utterances as

> The see may never be so still,
> That with a little wind it nil
> Overwhelme and turne also,
> As it were wood, in wawis go.

For the rest, it is the exhilaration and high promise of the early days of the year, sorting well with his large and generous outlook upon human affairs, that Chaucer gathers into his song. Nature is not for him to analyse or to relate to his own soul. There is sorrow in the world, but he cannot contemplate it long. There is gloom and decay in nature, but these too he will not consider. Spring, the season of sweet sanity, is for him, and he remembers winter only as the vanquished of the new summer :

# CHAUCER: THE POET OF SPRING

Now welcome somer, with thy sonne softe,
That hast this wintres weders over-shake,
And driven away the longe nightes blake!

Seynt Valentyn, that art ful hy on lofte;
Thus singen smale foules for they sake—
　　Now welcom somer, with they sonne softe,
　　That hast this wintres weders over-shake.

Wel han they cause for to gladen ofte,
Sith ech of hem recovered hath his make;
Ful blissful may they singen whan they wake,
　　Now welcom somer, with thy sonne softe,
　　That hast this wintres weders over-shake,
　　And driven away the longe nightes blake.

# PHILIP SIDNEY

SIDNEY'S reputation as a poet may be said to rest chiefly on his sonnet sequence, *Astrophel and Stella*. Although in the *Arcadia* and amongst the miscellaneous work may be found isolated poems of great beauty, it was when writing *Astrophel and Stella* that the poet set aside all thought of his ill-considered theories of poetical technique—of which more hereafter—ceased to think of verse-making as a pleasant and polished accomplishment, and wrote with fire and passion as all true poets write, to ease his mind. The few comments which may be offered concerning this his greatest work may be held to apply, broadly speaking, to his less considerable achievements. At the outset, however, it will be well to glance briefly at the state of English poetry at the time when Sidney was writing, and incidentally to clear away such obstacles as his classical experiments which may hinder us

# PHILIP SIDNEY

in the consideration of his most notable contribution to poetical literature.

We of to-day, looking back on our great line of poets, from Chaucer to Swinburne, find it not a little difficult to adjust our point of view to that of a man born in 1554. Such a one, given the guiding instinct, would see in Chaucer the first and solitary great English poet, succeeded by indifferent imitators, and darkness until the publication of *Tottel's Miscellany* in 1557. This collection consisted chiefly of the poems of Sir Thomas Wyatt (1503–1542) and Henry Howard, Earl of Surrey (1516–1547). These poems were remarkable in two ways: for their individual excellence and inspiration, and for the new turn which they gave to the craft of verse-making in England. Of the comparative merits of Wyatt and Surrey, and the respective shares they took in the new movement, it is not necessary to speak here. When they began to write the influence of Chaucer had deteriorated through ill-usage at the hands of many inept disciples, until it had become, for practical purposes, almost negligible. The poet writing to-day, with the accumulated experience and example of half a hundred great names ready to his hand, can scarcely reconstruct the position of the man who feels the impulse to sing, and yet lacks the inspiration and aid of a single great voice before him. The poet, indeed, is no common pick-purse or imitator, yet when he can boast of noble ancestry, his song will of necessity bear in some measure the impress and character of his descent. That this should be so is, of course, both natural and right. Wyatt and Surrey, however, wrote under no such auspicious circumstances. To their own poetical forbears they could look for but little guidance, and they turned to the poets of Italy and France. From them they borrowed the sonnet form, which had been popularised in an extraordinary manner by Petrarch, and introduced it into England. Modifying it in structure and arrangement, they adhered to certain fundamental requirements, and in so doing they evolved a certain degree of order out of the chaos into which English verse had fallen. The chastening influence of this self-imposed bondage, moreover, brought a new music and shapeliness into their less regulated lyrical work. To anything like full understanding of their craft they did not, of course, attain, but they left behind them many things of great value in themselves, and they set up for future and completer use the framework of a new and great tradition.

Sidney naturally came under the influence of these two men, and, partly through them, under that of their sources, the Italian and French sonneteers. He was not content, however, to leave the poetical revolution exactly where he had found it, and with Spenser, his senior by two years, and Gabriel Harvey, he conceived the idea of introducing classical metres into English verse. He, too, realised that some reform was called for, and considered that no better method could be adopted than that employed in the masterpieces of the ancients. The result was a woeful proof of the futility of attempting to impose the manner and possibilities of one language on another. That the experiment was an unqualified failure is no matter for wonder; that two such men as Spenser and Sidney should have discussed it seriously, is. Fortunately Spenser learnt to laugh at the whole question, and Sidney to discount it by his practice.

## PROSE PAPERS

The point need not be carried further. There is, however, another aspect of this question of foreign influence which is of the utmost importance. Sidney—and this consideration applies to the whole group of Elizabethan sonneteers—in going to foreign models for guidance in the matter of form, carried away with him not a little of their substance. Modern scholarship has shown these predatory excursions to have been both frequent and considerable in extent. It has, in a way, proved its case up to the hilt, by advancing numberless instances where an image or whole phrase has been appropriated without a qualm. In some cases, indeed, a complete sonnet is little more than a fairly close translation, and Thomas Watson, at least, admitted openly that his sequence of irregular stanzas, *The Tears of Fancy*, was no more than this. In Sidney's case, however, as in that of most of his contemporaries, the work is set before us as being original, and a decision as to whether this claim is or is not to be allowed, is obviously of great moment. *Astrophel and Stella* being a love poem, the first thing to be done when it is submitted to our judgment is to enquire

## PHILIP SIDNEY

whether it be sincere. The writers who have so convincingly denoted the debt of the Elizabethans to foreign models in form and stray—or even numerous—expressions and images, have directed us into an interesting field of poetical history. When, however, from these ascertained facts they proceed to draw deductions which set aside all the claims which the poet makes as being most essential to his function, dissent becomes imperative. We are told that these sonnets are no more than a clever exercise, displaying here and there a pretty fancy and a delicate ear for a musical phrase, having for their substance hearsay and conventional attitudes, devoid of all inventiveness, passion, and conviction. That they are, in short, written precisely as poetry should not be written, from the head and not from the heart. At this stage of the enquiry we come to something beyond the application of judicial learning to facts, we come to the application of our feeling to that of the poet.

> When my good angel guides me to the place
> Where all my good I do in Stella see,
> That heav'n of joys throws only down on me
> Thund'ring disdains and lightenings of disgrace;

## PROSE PAPERS

> But when the rugged'st step of Fortune's race
> Makes me fall from her sight, then sweetly she
> With words wherein the Muses' treasures be,
> Shows love and pity to my absent case.
> Now I, wit-beaten long by hardest fate,
> So dull am, that I cannot look into
> The ground of this fierce love and lovely hate.
> Then, some good body, tell me how I do,
> Whose presence absence, absence presence is;
> Blest in my curse, and cursed in my bliss.

If writing like that is artificial, it is an artificiality the secret of which has been lost, for utterance of the kind only rises to-day from the deep wells of emotion.

In this connection there is, however, a special circumstance in Sidney's case to be considered. The Stella of the sonnets was Penelope Devereux, daughter of the Earl of Essex. So much is clear from both external and internal evidence. The known facts of her history, in so far as it affects her relations with Sidney, may be told briefly. They met when he was just over twenty years of age, she barely thirteen. Shortly afterwards there was talk of a match, favoured by the parents on both sides, concerning which the parties chiefly interested were naturally—in view of the girl's age—not

## PHILIP SIDNEY

of any decided opinions. For no clearly assigned reason the matter fell through, though for the next four or five years it was still under consideration. It is clear that at this time neither he nor she entertained any serious affection for the other. In 1581, at the age of eighteen, Penelope married Lord Rich, from whom she was ultimately divorced to become the wife of the Earl of Devonshire, after having been that nobleman's mistress for some years. That her first marriage was unhappy is evident, and the conclusions drawn from these scanty premises are usually somewhat as follows:

Sidney, we are told, really loved Penelope from the first, but, being in no hurry to marry, let year after year go by without taking definite steps. Further, distracted by his court and official duties and his interests at Penshurst and Wilton, he was less ardent in his wooing than the lady desired. At length, partly out of pique, partly out of desperation, she married Lord Rich, and this event came to her old lover in the nature of a catastrophe. That which he could long since have had for the taking was now beyond his reach, and his desire was quickened and increased tenfold. His pent-up passion at length broke from its silence, and poured itself out in song. Then come new critics and very justly observe that all this is improbable in the extreme. That we know enough of Sidney's character not to believe that had he truly loved Penelope he would have dallied and made a fool both of himself and her. That he was a man of singularly clear judgment and self-knowledge, and that had his will been to marry this girl he would have given it effect. In demolishing one indefensible position, however, they proceed, I think, to set themselves up in another. Sidney did not, as is shown by the facts, they say, bear any sincere devotion to Penelope. Nevertheless this same Penelope is the object of the passionate declarations of the sonnets, and, therefore, the sonnets themselves are insincere, and become merely the ingenious display of a considerable poetic talent. In order effectively to cut off our retreat in all directions, they urge that if by any means the sonnets can be shown to be sincere, then they are certainly shown to be immoral, inasmuch as the object of these amorous protestations was a married woman. And so we have this elusive question of a poet's

## PHILIP SIDNEY

creativeness reduced to the most matter-of-fact rule-of-thumb that could be desired.

It may be granted at once that scattered through the sonnets are many signs of the poet's debt to his sources in more than actual structure ; that an idea is not infrequently taken from Petrarch or his followers. Further, that superficially they bear indisputable evidence of having been written for Lady Rich, the historical personage of whom we have a more or less complete record ; and lastly, that they are adorned or marred throughout by the conceits and extravagances which were the poetic fashion of the age. Then let us read the sequence carefully, and undisturbed by the hundred jarring theories as to its biographical interpretation, and we shall, I think, come to a decision which it is inconceivable could have at any time been overlooked. Poetic truth is a greater thing than the truth of courts and schools, and the sign of poetic truth is written large over the pages of *Astrophel and Stella*. A poet does not make a pretence of purging his soul for the entertainment of his fellows, nor does he use his poetry as a catalogue wherein to record the facts of his life. Sidney was in love.

With whom is a question that does not concern us in the least ; in all probability—it is indeed probable to the point of certainty—it was with none but an ideal of his own. As a framework upon which to build his ideal he chose Penelope Rich, and so the ideal became invested with certain of the qualities and circumstances of the material woman.

To suppose that the object of a poet's love and worship is either a definite being possessed of certain known attributes, or else a mere unsubstantial unreality from which he can gather no inspiration and support, is utterly to misunderstand both the poet and his poetry. It is a common thing to laugh lightly at the idea of a man being in love with love. The state is generally regarded as being incidental to nonage, a youthful abnormality that will burn itself out rapidly and finally. The truth is that many men and all poets are in love with love till the end of their days. The poet may be united to one woman and faithful to her, or he may from time to time fall under the spell of many, but, however this may be, he will create for his inmost need an ideal transcending his earthly love,

## PHILIP SIDNEY

fashioned indeed out of the material and suggestion of this love, but wrought into perfection on the anvil of his own imagination. Shelley we know wove *Epipsychidion* out of his acquaintance with Emilia Viviani, but Mary Shelley was wise enough to understand that the poem was the poet's creation. Tennyson wrote *In Memoriam*, and therein made Hallam a more supreme type of the friend than any man could ever be of himself; and was the Beatrice of Dante's song the daughter of a Florentine citizen? These reflections do not, of course, detract one whit from the honour and power of womanhood, but they do remind us of the danger and folly of attempting to reduce the poet's creation to the proportions of biographical fact. The material that a woman brings the poet upon which to build may be great or small; in Sidney's case it was probably slight, but it was sufficient for his purpose. Out of it he wrought a glowing passion of song, which may be hopelessly bewildering if we attempt to read it in the light of dates and records, but which becomes gracious and clear if we pass it through the fire of the imagination.

## PROSE PAPERS

I do not for a moment suggest that this idealisation by the poet of his love determines the existence of the physical side of his passion; on the other hand, the imaginative love of the poet is complete in every way. It is quite possible that some of the incidents of *Astrophel and Stella* referred to particular occurrences—for example, the meeting described in the fourth song. The important point to bear in mind is that the essential truth of these things is not in the least affected by the consideration as to whether they had or had not their counterpart in actual physical occurrences. Love is both of the flesh and of the spirit, and such is the love of which Sidney sings from a full store of imaginative experience. It is not for us to demand that this experience shall coincide with his diary.

*Astrophel and Stella* was first published by Thomas Newman, without authority, in 1591, that is to say five years after Sidney's death. It is clear from the Preface that the poems had long been in circulation in manuscript, but there is nothing to show that the poet himself had ever prepared them in any way for the press. In view of this circum-

## PHILIP SIDNEY

stance their freedom from obscurities is remarkable, no less than their singular smoothness and polish. It must be remembered that no poet of magnitude had arisen between Surrey and Sidney, and the technical advance beyond *Tottel's Miscellany* is enormous. It is possible, perhaps, that Sidney had seen some of Spenser's sonnets which were to be published in 1595 under the title of *Amoretti*, but, even so, they would not be sufficiently in perspective at the time to exercise any profound influence, however apparent their beauty might be. And, moreover, Sidney need not fear comparison with any other Elizabethan sonneteer save Shakespeare. The epithet "sugared," so commonly applied by critics of those days to contemporary poetry, has with us fallen into discredit as implying superfluous ornament and mere prettiness. When it was used it meant, precisely, sweet, and it was applied to Sidney's verse with perfect justice. In the whole sequence it would be difficult to pick out a score of halting lines, and this, when we remember the state in which the poet found English versification, is extraordinary. The sonnet form as he uses it is a compromise between the pure

Italian type and the English type, as used and made finally distinctive by Shakespeare. In the octave he generally adopts the Petrarchan rhyme scheme *a b b a   a b b a*, with the occasional variation—*a b a b   a b a b*. He never departs from the rule that the octave shall contain but two rhymes. In the sextet he is less regular, in most instances making use of the final couplet, and allowing himself any sequence for his three rhymes. Thus he observes the Italian arrangement of the octave and limitation to five rhymes in all, but generally infringes the rule of the sextet. It is not without interest to trace the descent of the sonnet from Petrarch to Shakespeare in this manner, using as illustration the type most generally used in each case :

| | | | |
|---|---|---|---|
| Petrarch | *a b b a* | *a b b a* | *c d e c d e* |
| Sidney | *a b b a* | *a b b a* | *c d c d e e* or *c c d e e d* |
| Spenser | *a b a b* | *b c b c* | *c d c d e e* |
| Shakespeare | *a b a b* | *c d c d* | *e f e f g g* |

A great deal of critical discussion has arisen as to the æsthetic value of these varying forms. What appears to be the root intention of the sonnet, namely, that the close of the octave should carry the tide of feeling and expression to its highest and most commanding point, and that this should find a more or less subdued lapse in the sextet, was of course defeated by the Elizabethan use of the final couplet, which serves rather to emphasise than repress the last note. In similar manner the latitude allowed in the number of rhymes in the English sonnet operates against that unity and conciseness which is properly characteristic of the form. It must be allowed that, all things considered, the Petrarchan type, with its rigid exclusion of all diffuseness, its recurrent beat, and its subtle arrangement of the sextet, whereby the rhymes are so placed as to avoid too great a sweetness and yet are just evident enough to satisfy the ear, is best fitted to lend the sonnet that dignity and lofty economy of expression which place it in poetry as a thing apart. At the same time dogmatism here, as in all things critical, is speedily confronted with its own folly. Mr. Harold H. Child, in touching upon one of the points above mentioned, sums up the whole question in a single observation:

"But the final couplet," he says, "has been

used so freely and to such noble ends by English writers that objection is out of place."[1]

The same may, of course, be said of all the variations and licenses to which I have alluded.

The only other observation to be made in the matter of the prosody of *Astrophel and Stella* is that Sidney in a few instances uses lines of twelve syllables instead of the orthodox ten. This is a transgression which it is not so easy to defend; indeed it is, I think, indefensible. The ten syllable line is as essential to the character of the English sonnet as it is to that of English blank verse, and it may well be said that on this point if no other the requirement of the form admits no denial. One has only to look at an example of trespass in this direction, say the eighth sonnet of *Astrophel and Stella*, to perceive the extraordinary effect of incongruity that is produced. The lilting jog-trot of the line is agreeable enough in itself, but as we read on and find it wedded to a singularly austere rhyme arrangement, we feel as we should do if Mercutio spoke with the voice of Hamlet.

[1] *Cambridge History of English Literature*, vol. iii. chap. viii.

## PHILIP SIDNEY

Sidney's vocabulary was both extensive and flexible. He had in a marked degree the faculty of investing a familiar word with a deepened significance, rather than use a strange or eccentric one. The opening of one of the most famous sonnets in the series will suffice to illustrate this:

> With how sad steps, O Moon, thou climb'st the skies.
> How silently, and with how wan a face!
> What, may it be that even in heav'nly place
> That busy archer his sharp arrows tries?

It will be observed that there is no word here which is in the least uncommon, and yet by their disposition and through the conviction and feeling behind them they take on a distinctive atmosphere and become poetical in the true sense of the term. This power is, of course, one of the greatest that an artist can possess, and Sidney possessed it in full measure. In point of imagery he is not so decidedly successful. He was in no way free from the prevailing vice of conceit-making, and he too frequently seeks to illustrate his statement by mere fanciful decoration instead of penetrating imaginative parallel. What he has to say he says generally clearly and in suggestive, well-chosen language, but he seldom drives his utterance home by any elaboration which he may make. To do this, however, except on the rarest occasions, is an achievement reserved for the greatest alone, and by the greatest is implied the few who are great at all points, and it is no discredit to Sidney to say that he was not of these; he may still take rank with immortal names.

A poet to whom excellence can be allowed only on comparative and circumstantial grounds is, after all, in poor case. If he is only good as a pioneer, or for his years, or for his station, he cannot rightly be said to be good at all. As a pioneer Sidney makes an unanswerable claim to praise. He stands shoulder to shoulder with Spenser in the great movement of English verse. His friend, indeed, attained heights which he did not attempt, but he shares with him the honour of introducing new light and grace and strength into the verse that had already been beaten into some comeliness by the poets of *Tottel's Miscellany*. His claims do not, however, end here. Apart from all relative considerations, and judged solely as a poet by the highest standards which we can find, he occupies

## PHILIP SIDNEY

an honourable place in our literature. His poems are worthy to be read, and are read, to-day for their positive achievement. Taking up a vehicle which was at the time experimental and lacking in any finality of polish, he imparted to it a sweetness which at its best has rarely been excelled, and he used it to give expression to griefs and exultations of his own experience.

# THOMAS GRAY

THE acute power of observation that Alexander Pope applied so admirably to the manners of his time and the foibles of humanity was not wholly set aside in his contemplation of man's spiritual life and the beauty of the natural world. A tradition, not false in itself, but false in him because he accepted it without a poet's conviction, was, indeed, continually set between him and the thing seen. He could not see a woodland without pretending to himself that he also saw it peopled by "coy nymphs," and a flock of sheep outraged his sense of decency unless it was accompanied by Pan. But, in spite of this imaginative trickery, he had moments when he came near to seeing the loveliness of earth with undistracted vision, and they are moments that afford a striking commentary on the essential weakness of his poetry and that of his age. Whilst it is true that the sublime is but a step from the ridiculous, it is equally true that the greatest poets, those who have most often encompassed the sublime, are also those who have had least fear of the false step that should lead them to disaster. They have not infrequently taken it, and been utterly unashamed, probably not even conscious of their lapse. Great poetry is never self-conscious ; however carefully it may be wrought, the care is a concession to the poet's desire to express fully the thing that he has discovered, and not to his sense of propriety. The profoundest imaginative truth in poetry is often embodied in an utterance quite unable to bear examination by common standards of fact. A level-headed lawyer, who carried truth in a nutshell, reading Shelley's *Skylark*, came to the phrase " Thou scorner of the ground." " Nonsense," he exclaimed, " the bird makes its nest on the ground." The besetting sin of the temper in poetry for which Pope stood was precisely this self-consciousness, this distrust of poetic truth, this fear of the ridiculous. So that Pope, looking out on to distant hills and seeing that they were blue, was troubled. He knew that they were really green or brown, in any case not blue. And then he began to doubt whether even in appearance they were quite blue after all, and finally suppressed the poet that was in him and wrote :

> There wrapt in clouds the *blueish* hills ascend.

Propriety was unoffended, and we were given an epitome in one line of the twist that did so much to devitalise the poetry of the age.

As if to emphasise the essential unity of matter and manner in art, this timorousness of spirit found its exact parallel in the form into which poetry was shaped. The prevalence of the heroic couplet cannot have been due to any conviction in the minds of the poets that this was indisputably the form best fitted for the language. But it was capable of a balance, a regularity, a precision that commended it with peculiar force to men to whom these things were of first-rate importance in their reading of life. Once it had been handled by a master technician, it was thenceforth easy to determine at a glance whether the versification was correct, and the appeal to correctness was sacrosanct. Any departure from recognised rules could be instantly detected : a most comfortable privilege to men who valued rule more than adventure. Rejecting blank verse as sorting ill with that elegance which was a plaything for polite society, the poets were not disposed to surrender those qualities of blank verse most suited to their formal habit of mind. The five foot line was established as the staple of English verse, and by stripping it of variety and lending it the adornment of rhyme they found a vehicle as rigid as their own perceptions and at the same time not devoid of authority. To have experimented with more flexible lyrical forms would have been, in their eyes, wilful folly, for flexibility meant a confusion of standards, a license that would have destroyed the simple code of reference to which they were used. The relationship of early eighteenth-century poetry in England to classicism is extremely remote. In great classic art, as in great art of every kind, the supreme arbiter is the imagination, and it was the radical flaw of that phase of English poetry that the imagination was subjected not merely to the reason, but to a reason that continually argued back to formal standards and not forward to discoveries. The poets were not even progressive in their science.

To praise a poet because he achieved in spite of great difficulties rather than for his achievement itself is to serve him ill. The external circumstance of John Clare's poverty adds nothing to the worth of his lyrics. We may be astonished at the spectacle of a penniless and untutored labourer adding to the store of authentic poetry, but our astonishment has nothing to do with our understanding of art. It is not our concern, in seeking for the beauty that is the gift of art, to remember that Milton was blind or Beethoven deaf. We may acclaim Chaucer because he shaped a language, but we love him because he was a poet, and it is by our love that he is immortal. It is the function of poetry to impart to us strong exaltation, to free our imaginations and quicken our spiritual perceptions, and if it fails to do this no plea of disabilities or obstacles will serve the poet. That he might have done better under other circumstances, or that he did well considering this thing or that, does not matter. The poet's revelation alone can move us, and his written word is the only revelation that

## THOMAS GRAY

we can accept. If he fails to reveal we may still be interested in the failure, but for reasons remote from the divine curiosity that leads us to poetry.

There are, however, circumstances that, whilst not increasing the positive value of a poet's work, may throw his achievement into greater relief. Thomas Gray, who was born when Pope was twenty-eight years old, holds his place among the poets because he had something to reveal, and with whatever uncertainty and in however small a compass, found fit expression for the thing that he had to say, and for no other reason. But he arrests particular attention in the course of English poetry because he was the first man of importance to revolt against the formalism of the poets of the age into which he was born. The distinction was shared by Collins, who heralded the great romantic revival with a note of purer poetry than that of the poet who is more widely known, but the two men were working independently to the same end. Gray certainly owed nothing to Collins; he might, indeed, have done so with gain. His judgment was not at any time as sound in this matter of contemporary poetry as his instinct. He worked away from the things that he praised and towards the things in which he professed to see no virtue. We find him speaking highly of Shenstone and Beattie and Mason, and yet writing to his friend Wharton, " Have you seen the works of two young authors, a Mr. Warton and Mr. Collins, both writers of odes ? it is odd enough, but each is the half of a considerable man, and one the counterpart of the other. The first has but little invention, very poetical choice of expression, and a good ear. The second, a fine fancy, modelled upon the antique, a bad ear, great variety of words and images, with no choice at all. They both deserve to last some years, but will not." But the denial of the false tradition by which he was surrounded was no less emphatic because it was more or less unconscious. Gray's habitual outlook upon the world was rather of the scholarly observer than that of the creative seer, but he had moments of genuinely imaginative vision, and his instinct impelled him to allow these free and not unadventurous expression. Lyrical verse during the hundred years that followed him attained a variety and colour that would have seemed even to his independent mind the merest vagary and licentiousness; but in his rather formally constructed odes, and even in the simple stanzas of the *Elegy*, he made a definite and memorable departure from the rigidity that was threatening to deprive poetry of all its suppleness and finer expression. In his diction he was unable to escape with any certainty from the constraint of his age. Poetry in his hands was still too often concerned with hearsay instead of vision, and, save at times when he gave himself up wholly to his better impulse, he was ready to lend his authority to the fustian rhetoric that did duty for style. We still have the " attic warbler " and the " fury Passions," " melting strains," and the " enchanting shell," and we still find poetry masquerading in such dress as this:

> What idle progeny succeed
> To chase the rolling circle's speed,
> Or urge the flying ball?

There are, in short, many traces in Gray's poetry of a tradition against which he revolted but which he could not be expected to overcome at a stroke. But there are, scattered through his small volume of work, many instances of the poet's determination

## PROSE PAPERS

to express himself completely and with indifference to current standards. He could rival Pope himself on occasion in precision and the sublimation of mere reason, as for example in :

> all are men
> Condemned alike to groan,
> The tender for another's pain,
> The unfeeling for his own . . .

or :

> where ignorance is bliss
> 'Tis folly to be wise,

or again in such a phrase as " leave us leisure to be good." But he could also reach true dignity of style, a thing new to his time :

> Nor the pride, nor ample pinion
> That the Theban Eagle bear,
> Sailing with supreme dominion
> Thro' the azure deep of air,

and :

> In gallant trim the gilded vessel goes ;
> Youth on the prow and Pleasure at the helm,

are notes for which he could find no example among his contemporaries save Collins. And he could, further, touch the pure simplicity of manner that he found discredited and rejected in the practice of the men that were then accepted as controllers of taste, and is yet the highest triumph of the poet's expression. He did this not only in such isolated passages as :

> The meanest floweret of the vale,
> The simplest note that swells the gale,
> The common sun, the air, the skies,
> To him are opening Paradise,

but also, with very few lapses, throughout a whole poem. The *Elegy written in a Country Churchyard* has the distinction of being one of the few excellent poems in the language that are really popular. The qualities that have made it popular have, of course, nothing to do with Gray's position as a pioneer. They are those of tenderness and of clear distinction between sentiment and sentimentality, of intimacy with the beauty and change of earth, all set down without affectation and yet never meanly. It is a chapter of simple things which once again have gripped a poet by their loveliness and poignancy, and it is by virtue of this that it has won the affection of so many men ; but it does, nevertheless, take on a new distinction when we realise that it was written at a time when these qualities were most grudgingly served by poetry.

Gray had not a particularly rich imagination, but he was willing at times to allow what imaginative faculty he had free play. His power of vision was not of the highest, but in his more inspired moments he was careful to allow nothing to come between his vision and the thing seen. It has been charged against him that " he never spoke out." The criticism would not seem to be well considered. He did not, it is true, speak often, and he sometimes spoke without conviction. But it is not the least of his distinctions that at other times, when he was really moved to follow the guidance of his instinct, he was one of two men in his age who did speak out. He was not afraid to put on record the evidence of his imagination. If Gray saw blue hills he called them blue and not blueish.

Wordsworth did Gray an injustice by placing him " at the head of those who, by their reasonings, have attempted to widen the space of separation betwixt prose and metrical composition," and adding that he was " more than any other man curiously elaborate in the structure of his own poetic diction." Even in his elaboration Gray was doing something to escape from a precision numbing in its formality, and, although Wordsworth rightly protested against much in the earlier poet's diction, he might have drawn his examples as aptly from almost any of Gray's contemporaries, who could not have defended themselves by an " Elegy" or the passages of perfectly sincere and imaginative diction that are to be found in the Odes. Although Gray was not at all times a profitable servant, he was ever ready to acknowledge the lordship of the imagination, and it was ungenerous of Wordsworth to omit this fact from his reckoning. Johnson complained that he was " tall by walking on tiptoe," but the desire to be tall was in itself laudable, and not always unrewarded.

The poet's letters are not only delightful in their revelation of a most companionable personality, but they also contain many passages that show a clear-sightedness as to the general principles of his craft. It was natural enough that he should be mistaken as to Collins, and confused in his judgments of the work that was being done in his own day, even that he should at times be disloyal to his instincts in his own creation. The influence of Pope was too great for any man to resist without some hesitancy. But as soon as he began to consider the abstract nature of poetry he did so with admirable balance and insight. His professed essays on the art are concerned rather with the evolution of language and metrical form than with the cosmic spirit of poetry, but his correspondents might profit, if they were able, by many swift words of profound critical understanding. Speaking of description, he says, " I have always thought that it made the most graceful ornament of poetry, but never ought to make the subject," and his letters to Mason about that industrious writer's work abound in observations that are worthy of a better subject. It is clear from these flashes of criticism scattered through the letters that he had a finer understanding of his art than, perhaps, any man of his age, however inconsistently he may have applied his understanding in practice, and although this, again, does not add to his stature as poet, it gives some new distinction to his place in the history of letters.

The chief defect in his positive contribution to

poetry is its unconcern with humanity. He peoples his poems with personages that are but rarely warm with life. Gray was not commonly fortunate in his choice of subjects. The Odes, which form the greater part of his work, each contain incidental and isolated passages that by their sudden rise to excellence of style or their clarity and intimacy of feeling are made memorable, but they do not command our interest either by their unity of conception, their sustained beauty of expression, or their nearness to our own experience. In the *Elegy* alone among his more serious poems did he take a subject that by its simplicity and universality enabled him to write in complete accord with the impulse that was in him for direct and unstrained expression, and it is the *Elegy* that we treasure as a complete poem, reading it from beginning to end when we turn back to it, not hastening forward for some rare glimpse of splendour that we know awaits us. In his lighter poems, notably *The Long Story*, he attained something of this same warmth. His humour was always one of his most lovable qualities, and when he brings it to his poetry it is some compensation for the naturalness and depth that we miss in the Odes save at long intervals; nearly related as it is to the quick humanity that stirred him to utterance in the poem that popular affection has agreed with Dr. Johnson in proclaiming as his highest achievement.

# S. T. COLERIDGE

WHEN the psychologist comes who shall attempt *An Inquiry into the Visitations of Genius*, he might well adopt, as the sole basis of his investigation, *Coleridge's Complete Poetical Works*.[1] We have them here in two volumes, admirably produced and edited, amounting to well over eleven hundred pages. By virtue of these, Coleridge, who was born in the year after Gray's death, and wrote his first known poem in 1787, takes a moderately distinguished place among the poets for whom we can only feel a certain compassionate reverence for their loyalty to an art that steadily refused to bestow any of its finer favours on their services. The eighteenth-century poets, those who were bound by, instead of transcending, their age, may not have been aware of their own rather painful

---

[1] *The Complete Poetical Works of Samuel Taylor Coleridge.* Edited by Ernest Hartley Coleridge. (Clarendon Press.)

limitations; but they were, at best, not allowed to know anything of the rarer ecstasy which is the poet's right, and to despise them is to despise a singularly unfortunate company of men. The good Mr. Akenside, had he lived a hundred years earlier, with all his desire and labour for poetry, might have set his heart dancing to some jolly song, instead of laboriously spending it on a forlorn hope; and even he made some honourable endeavour to bridge the darkest years that poetry has known since its beginning in England, with little enough of the poet's one true reward, whatever he may have had of praise. And Coleridge normally—save for some divine whim, always—is of this company. He remarks of one of his earliest compositions that it is not beyond the power of any clever schoolboy; that it is no more than a *putting of thought into verse*. That was the staple industry of Coleridge and his fellows. Through eleven hundred pages we find thought being put into verse; thought sometimes witty, sometimes dull, very often pompous and sentimental; but, save at one or two blessed intervals, never thought transfused into imagination and poetry. It shines

## S. T. COLERIDGE

in the gay little *Ode in the Manner of Anacreon*; it is elephantine in things like the *Religious Musings*; it struggles towards something rarer in stray lines like:

> And scatter livelier roses round,

or stanzas such as:

> And oh! may Spring's fair flowerets fade,
> May Summer cease her limbs to lave
> In cooling stream, may Autumn grave
> Yellow o'er the corn-cloath'd glade;
> Ere . . .

or it trots merrily as in the lines *Written After a Walk before Supper*. It can become amazing, as in the *Lines to a Friend, who Died of a Frenzy Induced by Calumnious Reports*, beginning:

> Edmund! thy grave with aching eye I scan . . .

it can perform admirable tricks, as in the epigram on Donne:

> With Donne, whose muse on dromedary trots,
> Wreathe iron pokers into true-love knots;
> Rhyme's sturdy cripple, fancy's maze and clue,
> Wit's forge and fire-blast, meaning's press and screw.

And then, when the technique has been brought under easy control by long use, and the philosopher has matured, it can reach true sublimity in *The Hymn before Sunrise* and *Dejection*. Coleridge made all the poetic adventures approved by his time, and told of them generally as well as another, occasionally better. He wrote plays, too, and they make up one of the present volumes. In these he was Elizabethan by intention, and remained sealed of the eighteenth century in result. The sturdy strength that gave even Webster the mastery over his most unconsidered horrors was beyond the reach of the author of *Remorse*, whose terror is the make-believe of a child. For the eighteenth-century Coleridge and his peers, the tragic clashing of the natural world and of humanity was not a great emotional ecstasy, but something of which to make a ceremony. They called it horrific, and were quite unmoved. Having none of the wisdom of imagination, they conceived the great wastes of tragedy to be a kind of fairyland, peopled by Shapes and Presences, who moved to a perpetual accompaniment of tremendous thunder. The external confusion of action that was utterly unimportant in the Elizabethans, because it had behind it a supreme spiritual unity, became in the

## S. T. COLERIDGE

hands of these men a meaningless end, instead of a riotous symbol.

And in all this our psychologist of the arts might find much to entertain him before beginning to write his treatise, which treatise would be provoked by certain poems that cover, perhaps, sixty pages of these two volumes. The years 1797–8 are curiously memorable ones in the history of poetry. A poet, moving smoothly enough along the appointed ways of his age, " putting thought into verse " with some creditable success, in those years wrote *The Ancient Mariner* and *Christabel, Frost at Midnight*, with its incomparable :

> Therefore all seasons shall be sweet to thee,
> Whether the summer clothe the general earth
> With greenness, or the redbreast sit and sing
> Betwixt the tufts of snow on the bare branch
> Of mossy apple-tree, while the nigh thatch
> Smokes in the sun-thaw ; whether the eave-drops fall
> Heard only in the trances of the blast,
> Or if the secret ministry of frost
> Shall hang them up in silent icicles
> Quietly shining to the quiet moon,

and *Kubla Khan*. Whatever achievement may be claimed by other poets, none can point to anything more manifestly drawn from a vigorous and enchanted imagination than these poems. Divine caprice has overthrown reason, and, line by line, we meet with adventures that none can foretell, and none can re-conceive. In accounting for the visitation, our æsthetician-psychologist need be distracted by no external circumstance. It has been suggested that Wordsworth's friendship inspired Coleridge to this strange new enthusiasm. It may, indeed, have helped to loose the poet's tongue; but it cannot, in any way, account for the miracle of the word that he was to utter. The best work of Coleridge's later years was a development of his earliest and normal manner and vision, with stray flashes of the wonder that only for one short period attained to clear and sustained expression. In 1817 it broke into one fitful gust in the eleven lines of *The Knight's Tomb*, and at another date we get:

> So will I build my altar in the fields,
>   And the blue sky my fretted dome shall be,
> And the sweet fragrance that the wild flower yields
>   Shall be the incense I will yield to Thee,
> Thee only, God; and Thou shalt not despise
> Even me, the priest of this poor sacrifice.

## S. T. COLERIDGE

Even at his great period, Coleridge wrote with no certainty of genius. The three or four masterpieces were written at the same time as ineffective songs and pedestrian exercises, as untouched as possible by the heady inspiration of which he had tasted. What is yet stranger, the two moods and faculties may be found at this time in one poem, even in consecutive stanzas. That any poetic perception should be capable of setting these lines in the same poem is sufficiently amazing:

> 'Tis sweet to hear a brook, 'tis sweet
> To hear the Sabbath-bell,
> 'Tis sweet to hear them both at once,
> Deep in a woody dell.
> . . . . .
> So they sat chatting, while bad thoughts
> Were troubling Edward's rest;
> But soon they heard his hard, quick pants,
> And the thumping in his breast.

But there is, at least, a saving interval between them, whilst the beauty of the second stanza of the following succeeds the ill-shapen doggerel of the first with perfect unconcern:

> And he had passed a restless night,
> And was not well in health;
> The women sat down by his side,
> And talked as 'twere by stealth.

## PROSE PAPERS

> The Sun peeps through the close thick leaves,
>   See, dearest Ellen, see!
> 'Tis in the leaves, a little sun,
>   No bigger than your ee.

Coleridge's visitation yielded him a small harvest of exquisite and essential poetry. He came face to face with song for one glorious season, and then, from time to time, he was vouchsafed a momentary glimpse that enabled his pen to touch the paper with something of the divine expectancy, but no more. Eleven hundred of these pages are as a prodigious monument, built in an outworn fashion, durable but dead. They are interesting to the analyst; they even have some intellectual excitement of their own at intervals; but it is all in verse that never sings or flies because of its own imaginative discovery. And the remaining pages—less than a hundred of them—are among the most marvellous treasures of poetry. It is a sheer delight to write down again such things as:

> The harbour-bay was clear as glass,
> So smoothly it was strewn!
> And on the bay the moonlight lay,
> And the shadow of the moon.

## S. T. COLERIDGE

And :
> The thin gray cloud is spread on high,
> It covers but not hides the sky.
> The moon is behind, and at the full ;
> And yet she looks both small and dull.
> The night is chill, the cloud is gray :
> 'Tis a month before the month of May,
> And the Spring comes slowly up this way.

After all, the psychologist would but waste his pains. It is not to be explained. We can only watch Coleridge during those two years with " admiration," in Shakespeare's words :

> For he on honey-dew hath fed,
> And drunk the milk of Paradise.

# THE BRONTËS AS POETS

## I

IN his introduction to this volume,[1] Mr. Benson says: "It may frankly be confessed that the interest of the poems is entirely centred on the work of Emily. If it had not been for the genius which her work unmistakably displays, the poetry of the other three would have sunk into oblivion." If this is so, we may very reasonably ask why nearly half the book should be given up to this other negligible work: why Emily's genius should have to carry this dead weight about with it, because the dead weight happens to be the property of her relations. And dead weight it unquestionably is. Of Branwell we shall have a word to say later, but of both Charlotte and Anne the plain fact is that

[1] *Brontë Poems : Selections from the Poetry of Charlotte, Emily, Anne, and Branwell Brontë.* Edited, with an Introduction, by Arthur C. Benson. (Smith, Elder.)

# THE BRONTËS AS POETS

they were not poets at all. The verse of both has a certain biographical interest, and speaks truly enough of the sincerity of character of two women who did work of lasting distinction in another form of literature. For this reason it is not insignificant, but it is already easily accessible to those who wish to consult it for these values, and we see no good reason for reprinting it in a book for which the only occasion can be its poetical quality. In all the pages devoted to Charlotte's and Anne's verse, there is not a line that has the unmistakable flavour of poetry. There would appear to be an exception on page 16, in the poem beginning

> Gods of the old mythology,

and definitely marked by a sombre poetic imagination throughout its sixteen lines. It is here printed as Charlotte's work, but there is an editorial note saying, " This poem has been in some collections attributed to Emily Brontë." It was first printed under Mr. Shorter's editorship in Emily's collected poetry in 1910, and we do not know that it has been reprinted since, nor does Mr. Benson give any authority for this new attribution. By every internal evidence it is clearly Emily's; if Mr. Benson can make good Charlotte's claim to it, he establishes for her a moment of genuine poetic inspiration such as never revisited her.

All this is not in any way to detract from the fine gifts that made so memorable contributions to the English novel, but merely to guard against the danger—evident from the plan of such volumes as the one before us—of allowing these gifts to lend other activities an authority that their own achievement does not warrant. When we say that Ruskin and Carlyle made a very poor job of their attempts to write poetry, we do not belittle their noble powers, and we can still be wholly grateful for *Jane Eyre*, while saying that there is no reason, other than those already mentioned, for printing Charlotte Brontë's verses. They have none of the emotional pressure that forces itself into rhythmic pattern of expression, no trace of the perfect selection and ordering of words that are the tokens of complete imaginative experience, nor has it even any share of the metrical precision and polish that gave so much eighteenth-century verse its own distinction without giving it the higher character

## THE BRONTËS AS POETS

of poetry. It not only does not move us; it does not give us the pleasure that comes of witnessing expert accomplishment. In Anne's verse there is an occasional note of faintly charming ingenuousness, but it is rare, and her claim to poetry is as little real as Charlotte's.

## II

Of a great deal of Emily Brontë's verse, very much the same thing must be said as of that of her sisters. It bears the stamp of character as clearly, and her character was the rarest and most impressive of them all. But in doing this it does no more than confirm, without notably emphasising, facts which have been evident from every word that has been written of her from the time of Charlotte's letters. Again, we have to keep our minds clear as to our demands. Impressive and heroic character is of inestimable value in the world's business, but if Emily's work did no more than bear witness to such character, her distinction would be a far commoner thing than it actually is. And there is much of her verse that does hardly anything more than this. We say hardly, since there is often, even in her poorest work, an undeveloped but not wholly uninteresting instinct for rhythmic individuality. The instinct is not very adventurous, not sufficiently so, we think, to justify Mr. Benson's remark that " many of Emily's poems are bound to appeal most vividly to those who have a technical understanding of the craft of poetry." Most of Emily's verse is not particularly interesting to the student of poetic technique, but it has just a touch of rhythmic independence, and chiefly in the practice of packing a line so as to give it an added fullness and rapidity while retaining the exact stress value, as in :—

> I am the only being whose doom
> No tongue would ask, no eye would mourn,

and :

> As they were playing the pillars 'mong
> And bounding down the marble stair.

It is, of course, a device common enough in English poetry, but its use does show a care for the capacities of verse not to be found in the ordinary rhymester, and in the hands of a master it is capable of producing such splendid results as Swinburne was constantly achieving. And yet Mr. Benson, as though to refute himself at any cost—since here is the best support of his statement about the technical interest of Emily's verse—curiously tells us in footnotes that she used "being" and "playing" as monosyllables—bēng and plāng, thus depriving her of the credit for some technical skill, and accusing her of incredible pronunciation.

But even this interest added to its biographical value does not endow Emily Brontë's verse with any considerable poetic significance, and most of it, which has no more than these qualities, stands as little chance as Charlotte's or Anne's of receiving durable attention for its own sake. It has, this bulk of it, a greater intellectual gravity than theirs, a more apparent responsibility; it has also an occasional phrase that almost thrills, as "shadowy fiend," and very often vague indications of an intention towards poetry, of the poetic energy hidden away in the mind but seeking release. But as we read on through the work of her earlier years, we find page after page of these elusive suggestions that fail over and over again to shape themselves into poetry.

> The moonbeam and the storm,
>   The summer eve divine,
> The silent night of solemn calm,
>   The full moon's cloudless shine,
>
> Were once entwined with thee,
>   But now with weary pain,
> Lost vision! 'tis enough for me,
>   Thou canst not shine again.

It is general, indefinite, diffused, made up of easily accepted imagery—all of which poetry exactly is not. The sombre strength of Emily's very character itself for many years could find little but conventional expression, a rather hectic violence that may well have derived from the lesser side of Gray. "Froze upon my tongue," "their deadly ray would more than madden me," "wild blast," "dreary doom," "frenzied thoughts," "frantic curses"—all these are from one poem, written when she was twenty. With the exception of some undated work at the end of the collection, which we may assume to be roughly in its right place, the poems are given in chronological order. There is, from the beginning, a development of the

# THE BRONTËS AS POETS

qualities that we have mentioned; but not until 1841, when she was twenty-three, do we find anything more than the suggestion that here is a sincerely intentioned talent that might in a fortunate moment expand into poetic intensity.

Then the suggestion becomes a reasonable hope with the second stanza of *The Caged Bird* :

> Give we the hills our equal prayer,
>   Earth's breezy hills and heaven's blue sea ;
> I ask for nothing further here
>   But my own heart and liberty.

The achievement is not yet, but it has come nearer. There is in these lines a new precision of statement, a quickening in her use of words, a tightening up of the symmetry. A little later, in 1843, we come to

> Leaves upon Time's branch were growing brightly,
>   Full of sap, and full of silver dew ;
> Birds beneath its shelter gathered nightly ;
>   Daily round its flowers the wild bees flew.
>
> Sorrow passed, and plucked the golden blossom ;
>   Guilt stripped off the foliage in its pride ;
> But, within its parent's kindly bosom,
>   Flowed for ever Life's restoring tide.

The hope has become an assurance. The poetry has not come into unblemished life, but that poetry is seeking deliverance there can no longer be any doubt. And in less than a year we have *A Day Dream*, simple, indeed, and not of uniform certainty in its flight, but showing an athletic imagination coming into its own. Then, as far as we can tell from the recorded dates, for another year, with the exception of a formless and unsuccessful poem with good touches in it (which Mr. Benson quotes in his introduction but does not include in his selection), there is silence, to be broken by *Remembrance*, with its superb

> Cold in the earth—and fifteen wild Decembers,
> From those brown hills, have melted into spring,

and thereafter we have a poet who is never sure of proving herself for long together, but who repeatedly achieves the note that makes her rank secure against any challenge. The poems we have named, together with *Warning and Reply*, the song beginning " The linnet in the rocky dells," *How clear she shines*, " Plead for me," *Self-Interrogation, The Old Stoic, A Little While, The Moors,* and *No Coward Soul is Mine,* and stray lines, such as

> It was the autumn of the year,
> When grain grows yellow in the ear...

and

> The herons are flown to their trees by the Hall,

# THE BRONTËS AS POETS

and this, as spoken by the wind:

> And when thy heart is resting
> Beneath the church-aisle stone,
> I shall have time for mourning,
> And thou for being alone,

make but a small gathering, but they give to the author of one of the most passionate novels in the language the yet higher distinction of having enriched for ever the store of English poetry.

## III

There remains to be considered the surviving work of Branwell Brontë. It covers but a few pages: in Mr. Benson's selection, which we take as being representative, less than twenty. Branwell's story has been told many times, and always with the same conclusion. He had a good deal of natural charm, and a character that was for himself and his friends tragic in its weakness. "At home he is a drain on every resource—an impediment to all happiness," wrote Charlotte, who loved him; Swinburne, with customary vehemence, calls him a " contemptible caitiff "; Mr. Shorter, in the admirably arranged chapter on Branwell in his Brontë book, emphasises the general opinion; " his memory now craves that of our charity, we leave it alone," says Mr. Birrell, allowing, justly we think, that " had he been well bred and trained, and duly kicked and disciplined, he might have escaped a shocking fate and a disgraceful death." There is no disputing the facts; Branwell, whatever allowances may be made for him, was a moral weakling, a disaster to his family, and he drank or drugged himself to death. But that was not the whole tragedy. From the evidence of these few pages, he also destroyed a poet, and it is more than likely that he himself suffered most in the destruction. In this matter there has been much confusion. In their very natural indignation with a man who repaid the patience and love of his heroic sisters so ill, his critics have commonly refused to allow Branwell anything of what Mrs. Gaskell called his " brilliant talent." " He did no more than write poor verses," says one; " of his sisters'

## THE BRONËTS AS POETS

gifts he had not a particle," says another. Mr. Benson, who insists as clearly as his predecessors upon " the catastrophe of his life," does well, if the comparison had to be made, to say that " he had a higher instinct for poetry than either Charlotte or Anne," though he does so apologetically. The fact is that in Branwell was wrecked a quite notable poetic endowment, and neither truth nor morality is served by refusing to acknowledge the endowment because of the wreck. It may well be that in any poet who has achieved highly and used his gift worthily and fully, the balance of character can be shown to be with nobility, but that a man may woefully abuse it is as true of this gift as of any other. Although we may hopefully believe that such lamentable wastage is rare, yet even the great responsibility of poetry may sometimes be betrayed, as it was betrayed here, and to relieve Branwell of the responsibility altogether by denying his gift, and so to make his tragedy commonplace instead of realising its last bitterness, is to trifle with facts. Save for a moment now and then, the poetry in Branwell was strangled, but when

## PROSE PAPERS

we read a short poem, *Noah's Warning over Methuselah's Grave*, the general level of which hardly falls below that of its best stanzas,

> Will you compel my tongue to say,
>   That underneath this nameless sod,
> Your hands, with mine, have laid to-day,
>   The last on earth who walked with God?
>
> . . . . .
>
> By that vast wall of cloudy gloom,
>   Piled boding round the firmament;
> By all its presages of doom,
>   Children of men—Repent! Repent!

and find in another place:

> But all without lay silent in
>   The sunny hush of afternoon,
> And only muffled steps within
>   Passed slowly and sedately on,

and remember that the man who could, in spite of himself, write thus, living until he was past thirty, left what amounts to no more than a momentary gesture in witness of the precious gift that was there for his taking, the tragedy becomes far more poignant than it has commonly been shown to be.

# FREDERICK TENNYSON

EVERY poet is both born and made ; that is a rule to which there is no exception. The instinct, the energy, the fearlessness for poetry are a man's birthright or for ever beyond his acquisition ; but the faculty of shaping these into the tangible stuff of art is to be created by work as hard as a navvy's, and in no other way. The self-discipline of the man who is loyally seeking to train his imaginative sense to the pitch when the faintest suggestion of false thinking or the smallest failure in a chosen word is instantly perceived and corrected as destroying the final balance of the whole work is, indeed, colossal in its severity compared with that involved in any other kind of labour. The reason that artists not infrequently break under the strain is not that they are weaker than other people, but that the strain is so much heavier upon them. The average successful business man, who is in the habit of thinking more or less indulgently of artists as rather a slack lot, would be appalled if he could realise the relative daily expenditure of brain tissue as between himself and the artist of normal productivity. The trained alertness that enables a man to juggle deftly with " futures " is mere primitive dullness beside the insight, won only by unweariable patience, that enables him to distinguish between a thing said well and the same thing said ill, between form and its counterfeit. Turner having himself lashed to a mast so that he might really see what a storm was like, Browning assimilating the English dictionary as an elementary primer of his art, Ben Jonson exhausting classic learning to embellish his satires on Elizabethan London, Morris adding yet another virtue to his epic by crossing Iceland on a pony—here are trifling exploits that may be matched in the counting-house ; but not so the severity of the daily vigilance of eye and brain that taught these men to shape their eagerness for life into great art. It is a ridiculous, but strangely common, fallacy to suppose that art is an easy enough thing if you have the knack of it. It is not. If you have not the

# FREDERICK TENNYSON

knack of it, there is an end of the matter; but if you have, then begins a lifetime of the most exacting labour that a man can undergo if you are to make anything of it.

All of which is directly about Frederick Tennyson. He died in 1898 at the age of ninety-one. Allowing the first twenty years of his life for preparation for work and the last twenty for rest from it, then he was a poet—probably a lyric poet of the first, or of a very high, rank—less, shall we say, eight hours' close work a day at his job for fifty years. He was a poet born, and never came within the most distant promise of being a poet made.[1] In this volume of selections—inasmuch as it is of exactly the same texture from the first page to the last, we may take it that it is a thoroughly representative volume—there is everything that a poet can demand or desire as his heritage, and nothing else. Here is all the material of poetry. An instinct for beauty, a heightening of the common charities and passions, a sense of unity in all the manifestations of life, the fearless desire for truth

[1] *The Shorter Poems of Frederick Tennyson.* (Macmillan.)

and a gift of quick and shining speech ; in short, fullness of life. But here is not only the fullness of life, but also its formlessness. The chaos is not disciplined into shape ; the man who would be, and by his birthright might have been, a poet, has broken an imperative clause in the contract, and has refused to work. The instincts, the thought, the delight, the imagery, the speech, all are incessantly vague, unorganised. And there is no such thing as vague poetry. Poetry may be difficult, so subtle in significance as to elude any but the most careful enquirer, but vagueness cancels poetry as certainly as 33° F. cancels frost. Frederick Tennyson is rarely subtle or difficult ; his verse does not exercise the mind—it blurs it. And it is precisely this missing quality of definiteness that work, and work alone, could have supplied. Mr. Charles Tennyson, who writes the preface to this volume, and, on the whole, writes it excellently, recognises this defect in his subject's work, but does not seem to recognise its full gravity. "Extreme abstraction" and "extreme diffuseness," when they really are extreme, can scarcely be said to be faults in poetry ; rather where they are

## FREDERICK TENNYSON

poetry cannot be. A great many people are full of right tendencies in their thought and instincts about life, but the trouble is that with so vastly complex a subject before them, their thought and instincts will, strive as they may, remain " abstracted " and " diffuse." It is to the poet that we look to clear away all this vagueness and difficult confusion, and substitute clarity and order. If he does not do that, he is no more poet than are other people, which means that he has as little reason for explaining his shortcomings in a book.

There are, it is true, remarkable qualities in this volume—highly exasperating qualities as it happens. The man who could write

> What do they there with lance and helm,
> And corslets that shake off the light?

and

> The banded sheaves stand orderly
> Against the purple autumn sky,
> Like armies of Prosperity . . .

might have come to be a very considerable figure in his art. But he seems to have been one of the men who are always too busy to work. His mind was occupied with a hundred things: spiritualism, drawing (there is something almost pathetic in the statement that his family still has " one excellent example of his work—an Italian landscape, painted in half an hour, on the back of his plate after breakfast "), music, sport, society. All these things are well enough for a poet if they are recreation and subordinate to his work as a poet ; but when a man takes to them all indifferently, as the normal habit of his life, there is an end to all hope of really big achievement. And so it was, for example, that when Frederick Tennyson turned his attention for the moment to the study of verse technique, he was attracted chiefly by the pleasure of building up more or less elaborate stanza structures, the sort of thing that anyone can do on a winter's evening if he thinks it worth while ; but that a poet only does to amuse himself now and again after he has learnt that the whole range of verse-technique, from the veriest album incompetency to the most superb lyric mastery, may be covered in a perfectly regular five-foot quatrain. Kingsley said of him that, " even in his most abstract lines, he often wrote with the neatness of Pope," which can only mean that he was sure of his finger-beats, since Pope's neatness was the

## FREDERICK TENNYSON

result of clear-cut precision in statement that amounted at times, indeed, to a poverty of significance in its surrender to formalism (as distinguished from form), but was certainly always far removed from vagueness of the kind that beset Frederick Tennyson. So that the claim amounts to nothing ; anyone, again, can beat out regular lines of verse who has nothing better to do. No ; Frederick Tennyson was richly endowed with a poet's natural gifts ; if he had given himself to the organising of his world, to making the shapes and rumours that were ever active in his brain biddable to the transfiguring power of a severe art, if he had worked, he could not have known defeat. As it is, we are forced to consider him for a moment with his brother. This volume suggests that the two men were pretty equally blessed in natural equipment, neither of them being fortunate in this way as have been the very greatest ; but one of them, with gifts enough at the outset to make such an end possible, achieving greatness and an impregnable place in his art by sheer hard work.

# WILLIAM MORRIS AND THE STATE

MORRIS'S essays and lectures on art and socialism, if they can in any way be thought of as separate subjects in his philosophy, *Hopes and Fears for Art, Lectures on Art and Industry, Signs of Change,* and *Lectures on Socialism,* have but one theme ; but it is a theme that he rightly supposed to be incomparably the most important of all the concerns of propaganda in these days. An enormous proportion of the people living under modern civilisation, so runs the argument, is engaged in joyless work—work that leaves neither surplus energy nor time for more wholesome employment. That is the master-crime of which we as a society stand accused to-day, and no one yet has found—or is likely to find—any semblance of a plausible defence. The psychology of the matter is complicated enough, but the root of the trouble lies clearly in the natural law that when a mind ceases

## WILLIAM MORRIS AND THE STATE

to be productive it becomes avaricious, and at the same time, loses its sense of beauty. Thus, when a man passes from the proper condition of his being, which is production, by means of acquiring control over the production of others, he will cause those others to make a great many unnecessary things without caring that they should have beauty—the sign of the producer's joy in producing—which, indeed, under this new and senseless pressure of demand, they could not have. And so, by a process which is quite direct and simple and only appears confused and indefinable because of the vast area over which it works, capitalism destroys the delight in labour, which is the greatest privilege of man and the secret of all communal health. In attacking this perversion of Nature's intention, Morris found two weapons to his hand—an active socialist programme and art. Of the former, an appeal by reason as much to the drivers as to the driven, he had no great hopes; nor has the prospect changed since his time. Poverty, with its attendant ugliness, is a great spoiler of the wits, and capitalism will not soon be ready to accept any argument as being better than its money. Such activity has its uses, but it is at best but a patching of an odd rent here and there ; and Morris, with many of his fellows, found in it more weariness than satisfaction. But his larger socialism, which was art, struck down to the roots, and there are many artists and friends of art—a growing number—who still believe that in his gospel lies the hope of the world. These lectures, given to working men throughout the country, exclude for the sake of convenience, in his own words, from their definition of art, " all appeals to the intellect and emotion that are not addressed to the eyesight," dealing with all those concerns of the craftsman which elsewhere he groups under the general term architecture. In this way, illustrated liberally by example, and developed in crafts-rooms wherever possible, he sought to move the workers to demand such leisure as would enable them to express delight in their work by making it beautiful, and so by a natural consequence to destroy the over-production which he denounced as the curse of competitive commerce. And all this effort was one in instinct with his own creative art—from his poetry to the designing of a chintz. "It is the province of art," he says in *How I became a Socialist*, "to set the true ideal of a full and reasonable life before [men], a life to which the perception and creation of beauty, the enjoyment of real pleasure that is, shall be felt to be as necessary to man as his daily bread, and that no man, and no set of men, can be deprived of this except by mere opposition, which should be resisted to the utmost."

It is a simple remedy for the ills of the world, one in which, in spite of everything, there is yet much strong faith. Yet how far we are short of its proper use the tale of these disastrous times stands in witness. For let it be said clearly and as often as possible, lest it should be forgotten again in these coming days when Europe will gather to the most momentous counsels of her history, that if there is one body of men who would have consistently and unanimously opposed the policies that have ended in this disaster of blood, it is not the churchmen, nor the enlightened publicists, nor the Liberal politicians, but the creative artists. It is idle to say that the artist is an unpractical visionary, incapable of rational conduct either of himself or of affairs. The notion is possible only to people whose acquaintance with artists is confined to gossip of or about very minor poets, and even more minor critics who spend their energies chattering in the unsavoury kind of salon. It is equally idle to say that the usual platforms are open to the artist, and that here he can take his share in the control of things when he wishes. His way is not the way which has, in plain facts, come to so terrible an issue. He says, quite comprehensively, let art be recognised as the most powerful of all authorities, let it be fostered everywhere, and so—and so only—shall you give men clean minds, and through clean minds alone can you beget in them the will and the courage to resist and destroy the folly of a few idle and mischievous brains. And if this counsel is once again swept aside by the men of affairs as a piece of pleasant but fantastic idealism, then quite surely the savage that is in the world will have its way again in due time in spite of all treaties. A Europe peopled by men whose daily lives were governed by the happy energy that an understanding of art begets—unless it be too oppressed on every side by

# WILLIAM MORRIS AND THE STATE

antagonistic forces—could never, it is not necessary to say, have involved itself in this desperate madness.

These prose papers of Morris's are a full and often superbly managed exposition of his artistic creed. There is, as he states in one of his prefaces, a good deal of repetition, as was inevitable; but on the whole they are, perhaps, the noblest statement of faith that any creative artist of the first rank has ever made. When we remember that the passion and clear-headed analysis of facts that went to their making were but momentary incidents in that crowded life, we can but wonder afresh whether there was ever an energy like to this. And yet in this splendid brain, full of righteousness and hope and imagination, there is an incompleteness. It would be more reasonable, perhaps, to say that the quality which seems to be missing was never tested. Its lack interfered in no way with the fullness of his own work. He saw a world, perfect within natural limitations; he realised it in his poetry, he preached its conditions, and, as far as possible, realised these, too, in his own life and the lives of those who came under his influence. It is a lack upon which we find a curious comment in an interesting list of his chosen books that Morris contributed to a newspaper symposium in 1885. The Bible, Homer, Beowulf, the sagas, folk-tales, and traditional poems were safe for inclusion—most, indeed, of the ancient and mediæval masters, but Euripides is banned here as by Swinburne, and of Virgil no more is allowed than, " Of course, I admit the archæological value of some of them, especially Virgil and Ovid." After Chaucer, no English poet until Shakespeare is named, and thence only Blake, Coleridge, Shelley, Keats, and Byron. And beside this list there is the significant note : " I hope I shall escape boycotting at the hands of my countrymen for leaving out Milton ; but the union in his works of cold classicalism with Puritanism (the two things which I hate most in the world) repels me so that I *cannot* read him." The " cold classicalism," in view of the richness of ornament with which Milton loads his poetry, seems just a word of hasty criticism ; but the " Puritanism " cannot be answered so. It would be absurd to suppose that Morris associated Milton with the sour-faced hypocrisy that used its power to destroy the beauty it could not understand without any wholesome zeal for the cause whose name it wrongly took. It seems to us that the quality in Milton with which Morris could not sympathise was a capacity for investing compromise with moral dignity. Here was a disagreement in which, without experience of the particular kind of circumstance that sharpens this quality, many of us would be on Morris's side. How many earnest and imaginative Englishmen, for example, had their views in this matter modified or reversed in August, 1914? Morris desired a certain state, and he saw it whole. In this, the chief, almost the only, purpose of his life, there could be no question of compromise. Therefore, compromise was to him simply the mean thing that normally all honest men know it to be. But Milton found himself faced with a great and terrible difficulty. He found himself, with no hope of intellectual escape, forced into the position of adopting and supporting means against which his whole natural manhood revolted, to attain something which he knew must yet be marked of imperfection when attained. And to justify himself to his own soul he could but say, and by a logical process of the spirit he was forced to say it: "My cause is righteous." Is it not the strangest irony of all in this dark day that we ourselves are forced to say "Our cause is righteous," since thereby we are forced to the acceptance of conduct at which, in itself, our whole being sickens? It is only direct experience of the mental state born of such a crisis that makes full sympathy quite possible. It is this fact that made Morris write that note. The greatest and most splendid fighter of his generation was spared the most bitter difficulty of all. But to-morrow his message must be heard.

# THEODORE WATTS-DUNTON

## I

IT has often been said, and said by men of perception, that the temper of an age is reflected more exactly in the work of its secondary writers than in that of its masters. Taking the generalisation at its apparent significance, it would seem to have but a slender foundation of truth. The masters are gluttons of honour, and they add to their success in directing the attention of posterity to their analysis of the elemental things of life, the distinction of recording, not deliberately, but implicitly and casually, the intellectual and spiritual habit of their own time more efficiently than their subordinates. Apart from their supremacy on more important grounds, Spenser, Shakespeare and Jonson tell us more of the underlying spiritual activity of Elizabethan England than all Dekker's admirable journalism and a dozen *Yorkshire Tragedies*; Milton and

## PROSE PAPERS

Herrick, set aptly at an angle, are the justest mirrors of the fundamentals of their age, Pope of his. And it is always so. We know the atmosphere of Mid-Victorian speculation and resistance and desire more accurately from the poetry of Tennyson, Browning, Arnold, Morris, Rossetti and Swinburne than we do from the more explicit records of many Tuppers. These widely accepted critical generalisations, however, seldom receive their sanction for nothing ; nor is the present one devoid of reason.

The measure of a poet's greatness is not the content of his art, but his art itself ; by the perfect shaping of his vision and not by the nature of his vision is he memorable. And the greater and more memorable his art, the more surely will its content be transformed from the workaday symbols by which it commonly expresses itself into new and more significant symbols of the poet's devising. It is the spirit, the essence of Elizabethan England that Shakespeare gives us, not the detailed circumstance. To the great artist his art is the most important thing in the world, a very purging and ordering of life itself. An obituary notice of Mr. Brown, late of the Colliery Board, will give us

## THEODORE WATTS-DUNTON

a great deal of exact information about an estimable man, but what would the world know of Edward King and Keats if Milton and Shelley were the only witnesses: yet by how much poorer would the world be in understanding of untimely death without *Lycidas* and *Adonais*? And so it is that the particular is absorbed by the great artist into the texture of his art, the outward aspect being changed while the significance is retained. The artist, in effect, brings his material into just subjection to his art, which he rightly believes to be more persuasive than life unformed and unselected. And since the intellectual habit and spiritual temper that distinguish his own age come within the range of his contemplation together with the emotional experiences common to all the ages, these too will, essentially, be wrought into his art, thence to impress themselves upon our consciousness in spite of the translation that has been made—indeed, the more incisively because of that translation. *Ulysses*, one of the poems in which Tennyson most definitely escaped the journalistic tendencies of his poorer work and asserted himself as of the masters, is finely eloquent of the character of the poet's own generation, notwithstanding an apparent indifference to it. The great artist is bearing witness to his age, but with no show of deliberation. After the great, however, there are two ranks of artists, defining themselves largely by the expression of their relation to their time. There are those, failing perhaps in their claim to be called artists at all, who can see nothing but an inert and shapeless image of their age, having no perception of its significance. They would see nothing in the career of Mr. Brown beyond the facts that he was educated at the town grammar school, joined his father, Sir Jonas Brown, in commerce at the age of seventeen, was elected . . . and so forth. In their work they substitute, in consequence, a certain explicitness of statement for comprehension, as when one of them addressed Matthew Arnold in a sonnet as

> The greatest educationist of thy time.

These people not only have no art, they have no vision. Of them it certainly cannot be said that they express their age, since they express nothing. But there is another kind of artist, not attaining greatness yet of wide influence and importance. His perceptive power is often acute, and it is directed upon the same objects as that of the masters; he too meditates upon the life common to the generations and the life peculiar to his own generation. His spiritual ardour is as loyal as that of greater artists than he, though it is less intense. He is aware of the necessity of inventing a new symbol to give authority to his expression of the thing before him, but his capacity for this invention is uncertain. In other words, although his purpose is active and not at all content with the journalistic record, his mastery over art is incomplete. His act of fashioning does not entirely absorb and transform the material upon which it works, and his achievement will therefore, in smaller or greater degree, leave the thing that he has seen stated but not interpreted. But this very statement makes for more immediate recognition of its subject than does interpretation, and so it is that when we consider such an artist, whose work has a dignity great enough to command our respect and even affection and is yet not controlled with the final mastery, we find the material in which he has worked finely emphasised without being re-created. And since his material is in part the character of his own generation, we are apt to say that he, more clearly than another, expresses the spirit of his age.

## II

Theodore Watts-Dunton was, perhaps, the most eminent example of the artist in this kind of his generation. The second half of the nineteenth century saw many poets who accomplished perfectly the expression of a slight but quite genuine impulse, making a durable music out of a not too ambitious adventurousness, but Watts-Dunton in his poetry aimed with fine earnestness at a breadth and power comparable to that achieved by his great contemporaries. Although the volume of his work as a poet is small, it is marked everywhere by the most serious intention and a diligent concern with the relating of a personal experience to universal experience. Now and again to sing consummately a secluded and delicate emotion was not at all his desire ; enthusiastically he set himself to travel the wide world of imaginative thought in high-hearted emulation of the masters, more than one of whom he could call friend. If time deals unkindly with his fame as a poet, it will be because he purposed far more greatly than many whose lasting if gentle reputation, built on no finer or even less considerable a natural equipment, is assured. *The Coming of Love,* his chief poem, is designed in the manner of greatness. It has notable qualities: a large instinct for bringing its landscape, much variety of event, and the conduct of subsidiary characters, to the presentation of the central character, Rhona; a deeply felt passion in the conception of that character itself; a frequent richness of diction and an occasional majesty of music. But with every grateful concession to an uncommon distinction of purpose, we have to admit that the art is not disciplined and comprehensive enough to crown so ambitious a scheme with success. The vision is individual, having something of the true discovery, but the imagination at work upon it relaxes too often to achieve the transformation of a fine vision into a great poem. To take three varying examples of this relaxing of the imagination :

> We two glide along
> 'Tween grassy banks she loves where, tall and strong,
> The buttercups stand gleaming, smiling, yellow.

The poet no doubt saw that the buttercups were all those things—tall, strong, gleaming, smiling, yellow—but categorically to state that they were so is not at all the same thing as translating the fact into poetry. The buttercups are there plainly enough, but the explicit detail fails to give them their due significance; for the moment the imagination has ceased to work upon the thing seen, which is left at its factual value. Then :

> And larks the sunshine turned to specks o' gold.

Here is an image which is an arbitrary invention of the fancy. When Milton speaks of the " marble air " he transcends fact in the achievement of imaginative truth, as does Shakespeare when he speaks of " golden lads," but to call a skyward lark, which in the sunlight appears black—which, poetically, *is* black—a speck of gold, is not to

## THEODORE WATTS-DUNTON

transcend fact but to forget it.¹  And this again is a weakening of the imaginative grip.  Finally:

> And merle and mavis answer finch and jay.

The imaginative laxity here is none the less real because it happens to be of a curiously subtle kind. When Byron wrote

> The mountains look on Marathon,
> And Marathon looks on the sea,

he was selecting from truth in order to create an image having a new truth of its own.  It is pointless to remind him that the mountains look on the sea as well as on Marathon, and that in turn it is not Marathon alone that looks on the sea, since the mountains do this too.  Byron justifies his disregard of these facts by a perfect expression of the fact essential to his purpose.  But to suggest that merle and mavis answer finch and jay as against merle answering mavis, and so forth, is to make a

---

[1] I need hardly point out that when Shelley likens a lark in flight to a " glow-worm golden in a dell of dew," he is in reality likening the influence of the one phenomenon upon the imagination to that of the other, with no thought of identifying the appearances of the phenomena themselves.

very precise and therefore very challenging reconstitution of fact that has no corresponding gain, in the image created, to warrant it. These examples of artistic uncertainty would not be important in themselves, but there are not many pages in *The Coming of Love* on which one or another of them cannot in some degree be matched, and they are indications of the prevalent inadequacy of the art of the poem to deal greatly with a greatly intended design. The art too often either refrains from translating its material, life, or substitutes for its material a fancied life that is not quite good metal. This does not at all detract from the admirable qualities of the poem, nor is it to deny the poet his dues for a finely spirited purpose, but it does mean that in a work where continuity in the presentation of the central theme is of high or chief importance, the defect, destroying as it does complete and persistent fusion, makes the final achievement impossible. The poetic mastery is intermittent and therefore, as far as the structural value of the work as a whole is concerned, non-existent, and the success of the poem must remain with its more excellent parts. Failures of this kind are unfortunate for a poet's report, more unfortunate, perhaps, than they should be. Masterpieces *manqués* generally get less than their proper share of popular approval in the long run even if they get more than their deserts for a moment, but they are full of instruction and far from empty of delight for those who care to consider them. Noble purpose frustrated cannot compel the admiration won by noble purpose realised, but nobility of purpose is in either case good company. Though it may be relatively poor in conspicuous merits, and though it may fail for other reasons, *The Coming of Love* fails not more surely than most of Swinburne's and Tennyson's plays, than *Endymion*, than *The Romaunt of the Rose*. And who would wish these cancelled?

Whilst, however, Swinburne and Tennyson failed in their plays for lack of certainty in dramatic sense, and *Endymion* fails because it is but the delighted effervescence of immature genius, and *The Romaunt* because it is an almost unguided experiment in a new art, *The Coming of Love* fails because a ripened and really adventurous perception could not command an art equal to its purpose.

And this fact makes the poet curiously expressive, in the more obvious sense, of the spirit of his age. Tennyson was two poets, and the lesser of these and Watts-Dunton represent the characteristic temper of their time more directly, perhaps, than do any of their contemporaries. Tennyson at his best ranks with the other great Victorian poets as absorbing this local temper into the universal significance of his art, but there were times when his imagination relaxed in the same way as did Watts-Dunton's, leaving the material upon which it worked more exactly defined but not transfigured. And this temper was a blending of the last glow of the romanticism of which Gray and Collins and *Ossian* were the dawn, with a new and vigorous sympathy with individual men to which Wordsworth had sounded the lonely but mighty prelude. The romantic revival in England, or, as Watts-Dunton admirably called it, the renascence of wonder, was accompanied by a great deal of perfervid and hectic licence.

> With haggard eyes the poet stood ;
> (Loose his beard, and hoary hair
>   Stream'd, like a meteor, to the troubled air)

as Gray sang of his Bard, and even Collins dealt freely in "shrill shrieks" and "frantic fears." But, in spite of all excesses, wonder was reborn in the work of these men, to be caught up a little later into the superb art of Shelley and his peers. Shelley's ecstasy is rarer than Gray's or Collins's, and it is more perfectly controlled into poetry, but it is still of the same texture. His worship is rather of a sublime than a familiar landscape, of the liberated spirit of man than of man captive to circumstance. This is not to say that Shelley was unconcerned with the landscape about him or with humanity; he was, passionately, but these things were not only absorbed by his art, they became in his imagination so purged of circumstance as to be magnificently incomplete. In the creation of his world he did not reject common experience, but he purified it so completely as almost at times to go beyond the interpretation to the change of its significance. And while Shelley was thus finding for the single spirit of romantic wonder its supreme expression, Wordsworth was amplifying it by an alert reference to the immediate life of the world at his door, and the wonder broadened in its range without losing in intensity. The heritage into which Victorian poetry came was thus dual in nature. It had in it the rapturous wonder of Shelley and the patient but greatly eager inquiry of Wordsworth. And the inquiry worked upon the wonder, subduing it beautifully, without destroying it, investigating experience more in terms of the concrete image and aiming at a subtler or at least more complex psychology in its observation of life, until Browning and Arnold with more in them of Wordsworth than of Shelley, Tennyson —at his best—and Morris with, perhaps, an equal distribution of the two influences, and Swinburne and Rossetti more directly in descent from Shelley than from Wordsworth, through the agency of their own individual endowments, wrought into their poetry the spirit of their age with more or less sympathy towards the one or the other of its two chief characteristics.

Watts-Dunton accepted his heritage eagerly and in its fullness, and since his consciousness of its nature was highly developed, and since at the same time the translation of his vision through art

## THEODORE WATTS-DUNTON

was imperfect, we have in his work a vivid and easily intelligible testimony as to what the heritage was. The instinct for wonder and the instinct for inquiry, testing and modifying each other, move through all his poetry, expressing themselves with an openness that is almost *naïve*.

> Young with the youth the sea's embrace can lend,
>   Our glowing limbs, with sun and brown empearled,
> Seem born anew, and in your eyes, dear friend,
>   Rare pictures shine, like fairy flags unfurled,
> Of child-land, where the roofs of rainbows bend
>   Over the magic wonders of the world.

In such passages as these it is not the spirit of wonder wrought to the purpose of a great art that we find, it is the wonder itself, not invested with new significance, but very definitely emphasised for all to see. And even Tennyson, in his more restricted mood, was no more precise in curious observation than this:

> O God! a blazing world of sea—
> A blistered deck—an engine's grinding jar—
> Hot scents of scorching oil and paint and tar—
> And, in the offing up yon fiery lee,
> One spot in the air no bigger than a bee—
> A frigate-bird that sails alone afar.

## PROSE PAPERS

while the very constraint of a passage such as :

> The trees awake : I hear the branches creak !
> And ivy-leaves are tapping at the pane :
> Dawn draws across the grey a saffron streak,
>    To let me read at sunrise once again
>    Beautiful Rhona's letter, which has lain,
> Balming the pillow underneath my cheek,
> While in the dark her writing seemed to speak :
>    Her great eyes lit my brain,

reminds us the more immediately of the analytical activity controlling it. The spirit of inquiry is here being used as material, and so deliberate is the use that it is at once evident. And it would be difficult to find anything in the poetry of the period illustrating more explicitly the interaction of the two chief phases of the period's distinguishing temper than this :

> The young light peeps through yonder trembling chink
> The tent's mouth makes in answer to a breeze ;
> The rooks outside are stirring in the trees,
> Through which I see the deepening bars of pink.
> I hear the earliest anvils tingling clink
> From Jasper's forge ; the cattle on the leas
> Begin to low. She's waking by degrees :
> Sleep's rosy fetters melt, but link by link.
>
> What dream is hers ? Her eyelids shake with tears
> The fond eyes open now like flowers in dew :
> She sobs I know not what of passionate fears.

## THEODORE WATTS-DUNTON

" You'll never leave me now ?   There is but you ;
I dreamt a voice was whispering in my ears,
' The Dukkeripen [1] o' stars comes ever true '."

Wonder and inquiry are very plainly written here. If the poet's sincerity were less unchallengeable or his purpose less single, the wonder and inquiry would be vague in their statement because they would be but vaguely apprehended ; if his art were greater they would be suggested by a new symbol of the poet's invention instead of being clearly projected, as they are, in their own image. The spirit of the age is veritably manifest.

Watts-Dunton's poetry has been praised, and with every justification, by men whose authority is undeniable. His friendship with many of his great contemporaries may perhaps have accented their opinion of his work, but it would be not only ungracious but wholly unintelligent to suppose that the opinion and its statement were more influenced by circumstance than this. Morris wished to print *The Coming of Love*, and the sanction of the Kelmscott Press was not lightly given. Meredith and Mr. Hardy represent an

[1] Prophecy.

attitude very naturally adopted by a considerable body of the genius of the time towards a poet who expressed so lucidly material with which it was so deeply concerned itself. Meredith wrote of a sonnet on Coleridge: " The sonnet is pure amber for a piece of descriptive analogy that fits the poet wonderfully, and one might beat through volumes of essays and not so paint him." The work is praised for its admirable " descriptive analogy," not for its art. And similarly Mr. Hardy says of *Christmas at the Mermaid*: " it seems remarkable that you should have had the conjuring power to raise up those old years so brightly in your own mind first, as to be able to exhibit them to readers in such high relief of three dimensions, as one may say." Again it is the vision rather than its fashioning into great poetry that is noted and admired. This is not to detract from the weight and value of such approval, but to point out the habit in which the approval instinctively moved. The indisputable evidence of intellectual effort and sincerity that this poet gave in his work could claim with authority the applause of men who knew the rare value of these qualities, and they could bestow it with perfect honesty and gladly without considering the question of creative mastery too closely. So long as the art was not worthless, and here it certainly was not that, they were eager not to withhold their gratitude for fine spiritual determination merely because the art was not correspondingly great. And other critics than these, with, in a limited sense, equal justice, went beyond them in praise. It has already been said that while Watts-Dunton's imaginative discipline was not perfect enough to carry a great poetic design to the fullness of success at which, by its own magnitude, it aimed, he achieved many notable beauties in brief. In spite of its failure as a constructive whole, there are many memorable things in *The Coming of Love*, as the spirited and deftly modulated haymaking song, such lines as

> Where golden shafts from out the quiver of morn
> Pierce the wet leaves and wake the hidden thrush,

and

> But when I'm dead the Golden Hand o' Love
> Will shine some day where mists o' mornin' swim;
> Me too you'll see, dear, when the sun's red rim
> Peeps through the Rookery boughs by Rington spire
> And makes the wet leaves wink like stars o' fire;

> Then, when the skylark wakes the thrush and dove,
> An' squirrels jump, and rabbits scrabble roun',
> An' hares cock up their ears a-shinin' brown,
> An' grass an' blossoms mix their mornin' smells
> Wi' Dingle songs from all the chirikels,[1]
> You'll see me there above,

and touches so admirably contrived as the return of the burden of the quarrel poem in Rhona's plea made long afterwards in her letter:

> Come back minaw, and you may kiss your han
> To that fine rawni rowin on the river.

And this fortunate management is to be found, in some shape or another, in many of the shorter poems. *Christmas at the Mermaid* is full of energy, with a swinging narrative movement and many finely visualised descriptive strokes. A passage such as

> He saw a child watching the birds that flew
> Above a willow, through whose musky leaves
> A green musk-beetle shone with mail and greaves
> That shifted in the light to bronze and blue,

achieves, by virtue of its style, the translation of vision into poetry of which we have been speaking, and although there is in the poem at times the

---

[1] Birds.

# THEODORE WATTS-DUNTON

same kind of uncertainty as in *The Coming of Love*; it does not here interfere so seriously with the total effect, since the design is much less ambitious. The poem deserves and should continue to enjoy the wide favour that it has won. With the memory in our minds of many exquisite moments in his work, therefore, it is not surprising to hear of so authoritative a judge as Rossetti speaking of " Watts's magnificent star sonnet." Had it been possible for Watts-Dunton to concentrate his gifts on the production of a slender lyric output they might have been more profitably spent. But he set them to the creation of work that needed a master's far-ranging art to encompass, and his poetic achievement suffers in consequence. His responsiveness to the great masterpieces of poetry and his intimacy with men who were adding to their number led him to a lofty and eager emulation. This liberal purpose did not prosper in its highest ambition, but in following it loyally he attained to a poetry that is often beautiful, profoundly interesting as a study both in its failure and its success, and dignified always by an informing principle of earnest enthusiasm that, in its kind, touches greatness. And it has a definite place in the literary history of the age.

### III

In prose Watts-Dunton wrote his widely-known romance, *Aylwin*, and a great deal of uncollected criticism. The reputation of *Aylwin* as a very remarkable book is not likely to be seriously revised even though it should cease to be very commonly tested. It has the qualities and defects of his poetry, but in a work of prose fiction these particular qualities are of the highest importance while the defects do not assume at all the same gravity. The power of projecting vision into an insinuating but reticent art is still faulty, the imagination failing at times to fuse its materials. The following passage, for example, is quite sincerely conceived, but it is unwrought. Two children, both of them under twelve years of age, are talking. The spirit of the thing is true, but the expression impugns rather than enforces the truth.

"Don't you wish," said the little girl meditatively, " that men and women had voices more like birds ? "

The idea had never occurred to me before, but I understood in a moment what she meant and sympathised with her. Nature, of course, had been unkind to the lords and ladies of creation in this one matter of voice.

" Yes, I do," I said.

" I'm so glad you do," said she. " I've so often thought what a pity it is that God did not let men and women talk and sing as the birds do. I believe He let 'em talk like that in the Garden of Eden, don't you ? "

" I think it very likely," I said.

" Men's voices are so rough mostly and women's voices are so sharp mostly that it's sometimes a little hard to love 'em as you love the birds."

" It is," I said.

" Don't you think the poor birds must sometimes feel very much distressed at hearing the voices of men and women, especially when they all talk together ? "

The idea seemed so original and yet so true that it made me laugh ; we both laughed. . . .

" The rooks mayn't mind," said the little girl. . . . " But I'm afraid the blackbirds and thrushes can't like it. I do so wonder what they say about it."

But this artistic incompleteness is easily forgiven in a novel for qualities such as *Aylwin* possesses. It may pass as a little idiosyncratic to-day, but it has always seemed to me that the first duty of a work of fiction is to tell a good story and tell it convincingly. I have the hardihood to think that the novel has set itself to many tasks that can only be accomplished by poetry. However that may be, *Aylwin* does tell a story, full of passion and observation, and it maintains its interest with admirable sureness. The faculty that created Rhona Boswell in strong vivid outline is here put to excellent use, and we become intimately concerned in the histories of many credible and arresting people. In its own generation the book attracted as much attention for its adventures into mysticism as for its more durable qualities, which, in their degree, are those of Fielding and Scott and Dumas, to prove kinship with whom remains the novelist's highest distinction. The mysticism and scientific ferment of *Aylwin* may well perish; the simple humanity and narrative power of it will survive.

A careful selection of Watts-Dunton's critical essays should be a feather in some diligent editor's cap. Long before he had published anything, his opinions passed the rounds of literary circles with authority. He was over forty years old when his first critical article, a review of Mr. Gosse's poetic play, *King Erik*, appeared in the *Examiner*. The work which he subsequently did for the *Athenæum* and other papers did more, perhaps, than that of any other man of his time to establish a proper consideration of poetry in literary journalism.

# THEODORE WATTS-DUNTON

That in itself was a great service, but it was by no means the measure of the work's value. He explored the principles of literature with a discernment of a very rare order, and a well-edited selection from his pronouncements would take its place as one of the most clear-sighted—though not necessarily most profound—books of criticism in the language. His best known essay, that on Poetry in the *Encyclopædia Britannica*, is a little formless in design, largely because of the necessities of the occasion. But his criticism is not chiefly valuable for its sustained argument or comprehensive treatment of a given subject. It moves in leisurely fashion, discursive and sometimes quite gaily superficial, but at frequent and unexpected moments it drives a shaft right to the heart of its theme. They would make a very gallant quiverful for the gathering.*

## IV

I saw Theodore Watts-Dunton twice at "The Pines." He was then eighty years of age, but his

---

* The posthumous volume *The Renascence of Wonder* is so badly edited as to be worse than valueless.

mind was wholly unsubdued by his bodily infirmities. He was full of a most gracious courtesy, eager for any news of the literary world succeeding that in which he had lived with so much distinction. The nature of his most intimate relationship with that world, his friendship with Swinburne, has been told by Mr. Gosse, whose monograph on Swinburne has covered the ground once and for all. But it pleases me to record thus briefly the unseared enthusiasm and alertness of the old poet and critic. He talked freely of the great men who had been his friends, speaking of Rossetti as incomparably the most forceful personality of his age, of Morris's eager and noble simplicity, of Swinburne's insatiable appetite for newspaper reading sorting oddly with the amazing range of his knowledge of literature, and of a hundred other things making for pleasant gossip. He was anxious to hear about the new poets, generous in encouragement, and full of faith in the future of the art that he had loved and served. He made no mention of having written a line of verse himself, nor, save for a casual remark that " many years ago he did a good deal of work for the magazines " and a reference to a note in a new edition of *Aylwin*, any mention of having written at all. Now and again his mind would flash out in some brief critical disquisition, praising Dickens, it might be, or attacking Ibsen. It was curiously soothing to hear this old man who had lived through a generation which if it was distinguished by great friendships was also violated by bitter animosities, talking with serene freshness at the end.

# RUPERT BROOKE

## I

POSTERITY, untroubled by the regrets and intimate sorrows of friendship, untouched by the resentment with which we cannot but meet what for a moment seems mere brutality of accident, will see in Rupert Brooke's life, achievement, and death, one of those rare perfections that attain greatness by their very symmetry and fortunate grace. It is truly as though the gods would have this man great; as though, having given him all bright and clear qualities of brain and heart, they were impatient of any slow moving to the authority for which he was marked, and must, rather in divine caprice than in nature, bring him to untimely and bewildering fulfilment. His brief life, with its inevitable intervals of temperamental unrest, was happy in disposition and in event. It shone with many gifts other than the great gift of poetry. Wit, the cleanest kind of chivalry, inflexible sincerity, and the dear courtesy that only the sincere man knows, courage and reverence duly met, intellectual ease and great personal charm and beauty—all these made his friendship one of the most treasurable things of his time. But they did not touch his life to greatness. Had these been the whole story, there would have been nothing to mark his life from many millions that have gone through the world, eager, beautiful, forgotten. His achievement as a poet, definite, memorable, exhilarating, yet reaches its fullness in a volume of work circumscribed enough if we set it beside that by which any other poet establishes his claim to greatness. Finally his death, noble as it was, was yet but one of lamentable multitudes, marking heroism if you will, but not greatness. For it is not lightly that we call men great ; it is only once in a while that we single one from the many who do splendidly and fully all that they might do, and say that he among them all is great. But with this man fortune was to be lavish against all example. Although neither his brilliance in life nor his courage in death could place him among the few at whose names the blood of generations thrills, and although his work, sure as it is of durable fame, does not place him with those poets, perhaps a score in the language, who, by the scope and volume of their poetry alone, assert their greatness, yet Rupert Brooke will be a name as surely marked of greatness as any in England. Only once before in our history, I think, has a man passed to so large and just a renown with so unconsidered and slender a warrant. Until April 23rd in this year,[1] when this greatly loved boy died at the Dardanelles, Philip Sidney had not found his fellow.

To those of us who see in poetry the perfect flowering of life, the story of Rupert Brooke will always mean chiefly the score or so of poems in which he reached to the full maturity of his genius and gave imperishable expression to the very heart of his personality. Nor will any profound response to his poetry be enhanced by the accident that brought sublimity to his death, either in those who knew and loved him or in these few who from age to age shall build his best renown. Rupert Brooke, as all poets, would wish to stand or fall chiefly by his poetry, and in the ultimate judgment of poetry

[1] 1915.

no external circumstance whatever has the weight of a single word. Not even the fact that the man who wrote the sonnets, than which after long generations nothing shall make the year 1914 more memorable, served and died for England at war, can add one beat to their pulse. The poetry that shines and falls across them in one perfect and complete wave is, as poetry must always be, independent of all factual experience, and comes wholly from the deeper experience of the imagination. To say that only under the actual conditions could these sonnets have been written is not to the point. Experience of the conditions is common enough; the rare thing is the genius of the poet, and we know that this will fulfil itself be the conditions what they may. It is well to be clear in this matter. We must not suppose, as has sometimes been loosely suggested, that Brooke, in answering a national call, was stirred to a new and profounder poetic expression. At the time when his poetic power was moving in its fullness, it happened to find itself concerned with a great national crisis. The intensity with which this crisis seized his imagination produced poetry which must endure;

also it determined him to take up arms. But the two results were not dependent on each other, and to pretend that they were is a sophism of the kind that he would scornfully have repudiated. Had he for any reason been disqualified for service, the poetry would have come in no less certain measure. It is intensity of perception that creates poetry.

Rupert Brooke's best poems are secure of the admiration of all who have the wit to praise justly in these things, and it is this renown that he would most have desired. But we must remember that the people who care deeply and with understanding for rare and lovely art are very few ; a few thousands, perhaps, out of the many millions of an age. It is only the ineffectual visionary who supposes that the masses of the people will respond directly to the appeal of excellence in poetry or painting, or even in the more popular arts, as music and the drama. The evidence in the matter is plain enough ; I do not even know that the fact is lamentable : it is a fact. But there are already, as I believe there always will be, great numbers of people to whom the name of Rupert Brooke means something, while his poetry, strictly speaking, means nothing. There are times when such a thing is unhappy. The interest with which people who are incurably lazy in their higher perceptions will regard a poet who is a navvy, or has no arms, or is mentioned by a bishop, is merely nauseating and vulgar. But sometimes a poet becomes celebrated among this wider public in a way that makes for good. The homage that has instinctively been paid for three hundred years to Philip Sidney by people who know not a line of his poetry, and scarcely an event of his life, is wholesome and springs from the better parts of human nature. And so it is with Rupert Brooke. His truest fame will be with those who love his poetry, but the many spirits that will quicken at his name, knowing but vaguely of a brief and fortunate life, a brilliant personality, a poetic genius which they will not be curious to explore, a supreme sacrifice, will quicken worthily and to their own good. Always there will be the false gods of popular favour, the charlatans, the panders, the crafty and unscrupulous flatterers of mob-sentimentality, who betray their consciences daily for a little unsavoury power. The people exalt without understanding them, blindly praising, as it were, their own baser instincts. But, blindly too perhaps, the people will also desire and from time to time discover some external symbol of the nobility that is in them also, patiently keeping the balance of the world. Such a symbol, clear, almost spare, yet magnificently complete, is the radiant, perfectly poised story of Rupert Brooke.

## II

The development of Rupert Brooke's poetic power was, it seems to me, unlike that of most poets. The early verse of men who afterwards prove their authenticity generally shows a great emotional force with little intellectual power of arrangement, and a weakly imitative craftsmanship. The emotion will commonly be concerned, partly by personality and partly by acceptance from tradition, with what we may roughly call the more generous normal instincts of mankind, as a delight in the natural world, the lover's worship, hatred of tyranny, the mere high spirits of young and happy limbs, sorrow for the passing of beauty. Of such things is the material of most fine poetry, as it is of nearly all futile versifying, and so it is that early work frequently tells us nothing of its writer's future. We know that the material is there, but there is nothing to show whether or no there will ever be the art to shape it. But in Rupert Brooke's beginnings there is none of this. The volume of *Poems* published in 1911, which contains work written as early as 1905, when he was eighteen, shows an art curiously personal, skilful, deliberate. It shows, too, an intellectual deftness altogether unexpected in so young a poet, and it shows finally, not always but often, an indifference to the normal material upon which poets good and bad are apt to work from the outset, and in the shaping of which ultimately comes all poetry that is memorable. Nearly every page is interesting on account of its art and intellectual deftness, qualities that we should not expect to be marked. But there are many pages where we do not get the real glow of poetry, and this because the content, it seems to me, often fails to satisfy the demands of poetry. It is true enough to say that it does not matter what subject the poet may contemplate, but there is an implied provision that the subject shall be one that grips his emotions, one, that is to say, that he perceives poetically. It so happens that this capacity in subject-matter for stirring the emotion to poetic intensity is nearly always coincident with a sympathy with the common experience of the world. A poet may write in praise of his mistress as freshly to-day as if none had written before him, but, although we say that he may choose what theme he will, we could not respond to him if he told us in his song that, while he loved his lady and her beauty and his wooing was in all ways prosperous, the thing that he most desired was never to see her again. We should at once know that the attitude was a piece of cold intellectuality, that it was against poetry in substance.

In Rupert Brooke's earliest work there is a strain of this intellectual coldness. It is difficult, indeed impossible, to say exactly what was its source. It may partly have been an immature enthusiasm for Donne's poetry, partly a concession to University preciosity, partly a natural instinct that was not yet coloured by humanity and experience. To control sentiment was a determination that never left him, but to control sentiment is not at all the same thing as being afraid of it, and at the beginning he was apt to be afraid. And he would often substitute for the natural emotions which most young poets experience and cannot shape, an intellectual fancy that he cannot have felt with passion, and shape it with astonishing skill and attractiveness. Poetry cannot prosper on these terms; it must sit at the world's fire, or perish. The most common note that we find in his first book in illustration of my meaning is the presence at love's moment of the knowledge that women grow old and beauty fades. The reflection is true in fact, but it is not poetically true, and so, in its present shape, it is false. That is to say, we know that, although women do grow old, the lover in the delight of his mistress does not realise this, and that the assertion that he does is not emotional passion of conviction but intellectual deliberation. Rupert Brooke goes one step further into danger; not only does he assert that the lover feels something that we know he does not feel, but—it is perhaps an equitable penalty for the first false step—he makes the realisation of a fact that we know is not realised in the circumstances, a source of revulsion, when we know that if the lover felt at all about his mistress's old age it would certainly be with peace and surety. It is only a detached intellectual attitude towards a thing fully perceptible to passion alone, that can suffer the illusion that the lover's mood is subject to these external facts. To argue that a woman does really grow old and lose her younger beauty, and so may forgo something of her power, is beside the point; the lover does not hear you, and it is the lover's consciousness alone of which we are speaking. In poetic truth, which is the strictest truth, the woman, living in the young man's mood, is adorable beyond change, and if the young man says, " I worship you, but I know that you will grow old and fade, and that then I shall hate you," we know that he is speaking not from his heart but from a nimble brain.

We find, then, in a great many pages of this first book, an instrument that on so young lips is efficient and enchanting against almost all example, yet playing a tune that does not come wholly from the heart. Never, I think, has technique reached so great a perfection without corresponding authenticity of impulse. Only half a dozen times in the book do we get such phrases as " rife with magic and movement," or " whirling, blinding moil," and even in the poems where most we feel the lack of emotional truth, there is a beauty of words that made the book full of the most exciting promise. Already, too, there was in certain poems assurance against the danger that this intellectual constraint might degenerate into virtuosity. In the song beginning :

" Oh ! Love ! " they said, " is King of kings,"

the intellectual mood, even in the love traffic in which it has been most shy, is adjusting itself finely to the clear and common impulses of mankind, while in *Dust, The Fish, The Hill, The Jolly Company, Ambarvalia, Dining-Room Tea,* and the lovely opening sonnet :

Oh ! Death will find me, long before I tire
Of watching you . . .

there is a movement, a perfect visualisation of image and a clarity of individual thought, that mark him as being of the great tradition, and endowed with the spontaneity that fellowship in that tradition implies.

In the volume published after his death, Rupert Brooke seems to me to have passed into full and rich communion with the great normal life of the world. There are three poems: *All suddenly the Wind comes soft, The way that Lovers use is this*, and *Mary and Gabriel*, that are just a little formal perhaps, by no means valueless, but touched with some literary memory at a moment when the poetic faculty was not as alert as usual. There are two poems: *There's Wisdom in Women*, and *Love*, where the old detached and ironic mood that was once unreal returns not quite happily, and another, *The Chilterns*, in which it has been transmuted into a gracious and acceptable humour. Also there is a sonnet, *Unfortunate*, in which there is a reminiscence of the old mood, but it is now treated very reverently and with superb psychological insight. For the rest we have thrilling and adventurous beauty from beginning to end. There is no more tender landscape in English poetry than *Grantchester*, suffused as it is with a mood that never changes and yet passes between the wittiest laughter and the profoundest emotion with perfect naturalness. The subject-matter throughout the book no longer forces us to dissent or question. It has become wholly merged in the corporate art, and we accept it unhesitatingly as we accept the content of all splendid work. As in all really fine achievement in poetry, there is in his choice of form a glad acceptance and development of the traditions that have been slowly evolved through generations, and a perfect subjection of those forms to his own personality, until a sonnet becomes as definitely his own as if he had invented the external structure. We find, too, that the early constraint, even though it led to a touch of falsity at the time, has not been without its uses. The common emotions of the world he has, after jealous waiting, truly discovered and won for himself, unstaled of the world's usage. His passion is extraordinarily clean, burning among all simple things, clear, untroubled, ecstatic. Except in the two or three pages of which I have spoken, we find everywhere an almost fierce renunciation of anything that would not stir the plain knitters in the sun, with an unwearying determination to translate all this common simple life into the most exact and stirring beauty. It is true that in one or two cases, notably *Heaven*, the image that he creates of this simplicity of passion is such as not to relate itself easily at first glance to the clear normal thought that is nevertheless its basis if for a moment we consider its significance. When the poet elects to make brief intellectual holiday, so long as he does so in the terms of his own personality, we should do nothing but make holiday gladly with him. And we may well do so at intervals in a book that moves in the high consciousness of rare but natural poetic achievement, alert with the freshness and daring of splendid youth, grave in that profoundest knowledge which is imagination; a book that will surely pass to vigorous immortality.

### III

The first time I saw Rupert Brooke was in the summer of 1912, a few months after his first volume had been published. The editor of *Georgian Poetry*, whose friendship with the poet will itself make a page in literary history, and who is to write the story of his friend's life, had invited some of us to hear about his proposed anthology. There were then but a few moments in which Brooke and I could talk together, and all that I can remember is an impression of an extraordinarily alert intelligence, finely equipped with both wit and penetrative power, and resolutely declining to use either for any superficial effect. I suppose no one of his years can ever have had in greater measure the gifts that can be used to make easily swayed admiration gape, or greater temptations so to employ his qualities: and I am sure that no man has ever been more wholly indifferent to any such conquests. Humour he had in abundance, but of witty insincerity no trace. Never was a personality more finely balanced. It is this that I remember of him at that first meeting, this that I—and all his friends—found governing him and bracing his genius till the end. It has been said that he had a strain of self-consciousness about his personal charm and brilliance, that he was a little afraid lest that side of him should claim too much attention. To answer the suggestion would be an impertinence. He was properly glad of his qualities;

also, he was properly careless of them. The notion that any such matter ever occupied his mind for a moment can be nothing but ludicrous to those who knew him.

After 1912 I saw him several times in London and in Birmingham. I find a letter shortly after I had first met him, sending me his book, another in November speaking of it and some work of my own, and " feeling much excited " about the new repertory work in Birmingham. Nothing more till March, 1913, when he writes twice, arranging to come for the night, and asking for precise directions as to where he shall sit and how be dressed in the theatre. We stayed up most of the night talking. In May he sends me a play, and says he is just off to America for some months. Then, in the summer of 1914, he was back again, and we met in London after a vehement letter bidding me to a festivity in any clothes, which is to be immense fun, and if I haven't a bed he can find me a couch. Also he means to stay with us again in Birmingham next week, but he will have been to the dentist and will not be fit company for human beings. But he came, and I remember we exhausted the complete theory of drama in a tea-shop, went to a promenade concert afterwards, and again talked till morning. Also he arranged to take Lascelles Abercrombie, Wilfrid Gibson, and myself in a motor-car to some quiet place where we could discuss *New Numbers*, which was now being published. A few days later the project is written off as "I can't get the car that week. My mother demands it on some nefarious political business. We must work out something for later." The letter ends with a charming message to my wife, who has been, he sees, "infinitely victorious" in some tennis undertaking.

The something for later was never worked out. In the last week of July we lunched twice together in a Soho restaurant. War was threatening. If it broke, he must go; I think it was said in so many words; it certainly was clear. He was still eager about his new fellowship work at Cambridge, but, as one feels now, there was already in the eagerness the note of foreboding, calm indeed and wholly contented, that seemed to touch all his words thereafter till the end. I heard of him from time to time, then came a long and graphic letter after the fall of Antwerp, at which he was present with the Royal Naval Division. "There was some affair at Antwerp, I remember ... a burning city, the din of cannonades, a shattered railway-station, my sailors bivouacking in the gardens of a deserted château, refugees coming out of the darkness. ..." Then, "not a bad time and place to die, Belgium, 1915." We met once again. He was on sick leave, and I saw him for an hour in London. He talked of his new sonnets, just written, of Antwerp, of the boredom of training, the great fellowship that comes in fighting. He expected to be in England for some weeks, and it was arranged that I should spend a day or two with him at Blandford. But he went to the Dardanelles almost at once. On April 23rd I was in London. The news that came on that day was the most terrible that I have yet known.

# RUPERT BROOKE ON JOHN WEBSTER

WITH the publication of this book[1] we now have the complete work by which Rupert Brooke's place in letters will be decided: the two volumes of poems, the letters from America, and this essay in literary criticism. Mr. Marsh's memoir, when it is published, will give the world a closer knowledge of the poet's personal habit and character, and add an intimate emphasis to the qualities that stand out clearly from his writings. But from the work now published a full view of his achievement can be taken. Of the poetry much has been written, and, on the whole, a fairly just estimate has been formed. It is a permanent and exciting addition, slender and uneven as it is, to the thing that of all things England has done best. No man could ask anything better of fate than to be

---

[1] *John Webster and the Elizabethan Drama.* By Rupert Brooke. (Sidgwick and Jackson.)

remembered as an English poet. Brooke's letters showed us an alert and companionable young man, tremendously interested in everything that came in his way, with just as much " manner " as is healthy at twenty-five, and stamped already with rare intellectual grip and honesty. Now he establishes himself as a literary critic, assessing a large and difficult subject with skill and a poet's understanding.

This book was the dissertation for which Brooke was awarded his Fellowship at Cambridge. The first chapter is concerned with a general æsthetic, and, while there are many striking and witty comments, we do not get very far beyond the feeling of a healthy impatience in Brooke with the generalisations that grow so abundantly in this field of inquiry. Then follows an historical *précis* of the growth of English drama in general and of Elizabethan drama in particular. This is excellently done, and, without pretending in any way to be pioneer work, it deals very clear-sightedly with one or two confusions of thought that have been a snare to writers on the subject; as, for example, the neglect of dancing and minstrelsy as sources of the drama, and the indifference to the necessity of training an audience, no less than the actors, as " one of the conditions of great drama." The ensuing analysis of Webster's genius seems to us to display what, in a world of imperfections, may be said to be a perfect understanding of the subject. There are details both here and in the preliminary chapters upon which disagreement with Brooke could make out a very good case for itself. He quotes the second line of Brachiano's

> On pain of death, let no man name death to me :
> It is a word infinitely terrible

as being " tremendously moving " while many people would say that it weakens the superb force of the first line, and that it was set down by Webster for the admissible reason that it would make the significance slightly easier to an audience. Again, his assertion that Webster's language " was greater than speech, but it was in that kind ; it was not literature " is but an indulgence in a heresy and confusion. Nor is he very happy in finding lack of concentration to be one of the characteristics of the mystery and miracle plays.

We should say that one of the chief difficulties presented by them to an audience is over-concentration—a lack of detail in proving the development of the drama. But these differences are few and inevitable. The essay throughout, both in its reference to Webster's art and its consideration of the general principles of drama, is full of subtle perception. The Elizabethan habit of summing up the particular case in the first line of a concluding couplet and of presenting its general application in the second, the folly of the views of an "industrial age" about plagiarism, the enormous merit of the "domestic tragedies"—point after point is made with admirable conviction. Webster, for all his strange gloom of spirit that was almost a malady, a thing almost unnatural and against poetry in itself, was yet among our very greatest poets, and this book is an honour to the poet who wrote it and to the poet in celebration of whom it was written.

But the chief charm, perhaps the chief value of the book lies not in its direct contribution to criticism, notable as that is, but in its pervading temper, so strikingly characteristic of Brooke

## RUPERT BROOKE ON JOHN WEBSTER

himself and of the movement in which he was so memorable a figure. The new poetry, whatever its faults, has the great virtue of turning again to the sharply defined and simple experiences and events of normal life. It has freed itself of what Watts-Dunton, in one of his flashes of insight, called "knowingness." It is a denial, not in arrogance or without respect for the thing denied, but quite emphatic, of the kind of poetry that seemed to say that twilight was the only time of day in which vision could be clear, that confused innuendo with reticence, and was rather consciously concerned with langours and the perfumes of the boudoir. This elegant detachment produced many lovely poems, and though its charm was always faint, it is in no danger of extinction. But a reaction of vigour and open windows was bound to come, and Brooke was as fine and convinced a spirit as was to be found in its ranks. He was one of the new writers who see, without any sacrifice of intellectual force or subtlety, the eternal distinction between yea and nay. He was not afraid of calling a thing good or bad, recognising that to sit on the fence, whatever philosophical justification it may have, is not to do much towards helping the world go round, and is certainly to be dissociated from all great poetry. And his book on Webster is full of this robust and positive health. He revels in the story of Elizabethan art just as the Elizabethans themselves revelled in the making of it. It is all eager, forthright, and it moves with a finely careless haste, knowing that its general bearing is noble enough to be able to leave the smaller graces to look after themselves.

# THE NATURE OF DRAMA

The function of the artist being, whatever he may practice, to cast into clearly defined form that which in life and nature is formless, to refine and distinguish that which in the common run of experience is diffuse and vague, the first thing which he has to decide for himself is the selection of an image through which he may project his disciplined perception. And let it be said at once that in all art of urgent imagination, this decision is not at all an inevitable one, but one of carefully weighed and sometimes almost arbitrary deliberation. For the governing impulse that is at the back of the artist's mind, urging him to creation, is not truly the perception of some particular fact about a particular thing or person, but a conviction as to some more or less generalised phenomena stirred to activity in his brain by his cumulative experience of many men and things. It would be idle to suppose that Shakespeare suddenly came across the prototypes of Macbeth and Lady Macbeth and then had no more to do to express their tragedy than to invent a suitable succession of events. What happened was that Shakespeare, from long contact with life, became acutely aware of a certain strain of tragic beauty in the daily experience of the world, and to give shape to his perception had to find an image through which to work. And the image that he chose was not the story of Macbeth but the characters of Macbeth and Lady Macbeth which he then set in an adequate action. So that we may say not that Shakespeare in *Macbeth* chose to speak of two particular human characters, but that to shape his vision of profound elemental agencies and emotions he selected human character as the image for his purpose. It is necessary perhaps to lay particular emphasis upon the distinction between this use of the word character as covering all fundamental human passion, emotion and impulse, and that use of the word which is made when we talk of the comedy of character, which commonly refers to

## THE NATURE OF DRAMA

idiosyncracy and to the particularisation of fashion or manners. The word character as we are now using it has much in common with the word idea— we are talking of the drama of character or idea. The same considerations hold, as examination would show, if it were to our present point, in all the arts, but we need do no more, before proceeding to a more detailed analysis of the image in drama, than to look briefly at the subject in the light of other forms of the literary art. In lyric poetry, the poet, again pledged to select from and define his general experience, commonly does so in a direct and personal statement, but it will be found that in lyric poetry of any imaginative power, this statement is not really in celebration of a particular event or experience, but that a particular event or experience is recorded by the poet merely as an appropriate and forceful way of giving body to some profound generalisation of his mind slowly built out of his life. If it is not so, then his verse is but that of occasion, and gives him but minor rank. In short, the event or experience which he sings is not truly the purpose of his song, but the

## PROSE PAPERS

image through which that purpose may be fulfilled. The image itself may here sometimes be so slight as to be almost intangible :

> O waly, waly, up the bank,
> And waly, waly, down the brae,
> And waly, waly, yon burn-side,
> Where I and my love wont to gae !
> I lean'd my back unto an aik,
> I thocht it was a trustie tree ;
> But first it bow'd and syne it brak—
> Sae my true love did lichtlie me,

or, again, it may be so particularised as almost to seem to claim chief importance for itself :

> Now Arthur's seat sall be my bed,
> The sheets shall ne'er be 'filed by me ;
> Saint Anton's well sall be my drink ;
> Since my true love has forsaken me . . .

but in either case, if we truly respond to the poet we feel the profound and universal emotion which lies behind his particular statement. Arthur's seat and Saint Anton's well, and the lamenting by burn-side and up and down the bank and brae— these are not the inspiration of poetry, but the means that poetry selects to shape itself. The nature of the image chosen does not affect the

## THE NATURE OF DRAMA

quality of the artist's work. The remote and strange image of *Kubla Khan* or *La Belle Dame Sans Merci* conveys poetry to us as superbly as the intimate and direct image of *The Solitary Reaper* or *Sir Patrick Spens*. But the choice certainly has a considerable influence upon the scope of the artist's appeal. The more familiar his image the wider will be his audience. And the image nearest and most familiar to man is his fellow-man, and the artist, when he chooses human beings for his purpose, chooses the image which of all makes for the widest popularity. Assuming that he is truly an artist, that he is sincerely a creator, it will be, as I have already suggested, the character of his created people that he considers as his image, but to give that character play he will commonly invent an action, and thereby construct a story. And so we find that of all branches of the literary art the narrative, with human beings at its centre, is the most popular. I would say once again that this popularity is in itself no indication of quality either good or bad. Supreme art may be very widely popular or known to a small body of people who add but a dozen or so to their number in a generation. That twenty people know *Macbeth* for one who knows *Samson Agonistes* tells us nothing of the relative merits of those works. We shall see presently how spurious narrative art has obtained an enormous hold upon the people, but for the moment we are concerned only with the most general form of true narrative art, that is to say, narrative built about human character.

This kind of literary art, because of the increased immediacy and scope of its appeal, from time to time attracts a conscientious literary artist, and a good, or perhaps a great, novel or narrative poem is written. Chaucer, Fielding, Emily Brontë, Jane Austen, Morris, Meredith, Hardy—these writers, I believe, choose the narrative consciously because it seems to them to promise the widest audience, and they use it without impairing their creative integrity. I do not believe that the choice is governed by any fundamental necessity, or that it enables a man to say something essentially impossible to any method other than the narrative. I do not, for example, feel that Morris captures any fundamental emotion in his form that is impossible to Blake in his, or that Meredith is able

## THE NATURE OF DRAMA

to explore experience that is closed to Montaigne. But choosing the narrative form, it is possible for the artist to choose both wisely in his generation and honourably at once. And from this simple spoken and descriptive narrative to drama is but a step. The artist employing narrative in its simple form reaches his public through the ear; his work is primarily intended to be spoken aloud, and we may reasonably admit that when we are reading we are essentially receiving by the ear and not by the eye. He conceives a character, and then to show us the character in being and development he tells us that his imagined personage does such and such things, which action is realised to us by the ear only. Delighted with the popularity which his selection of humanity as his image has brought him, the artist may now consider how he may yet further widen his appeal without betraying his creative instinct. And he will ask whether people will not more readily attend to and understand him if he enables them to use two senses instead of one in receiving what he may have to communicate. He will say, quite logically—his reasoning, as always with the artist, is subconscious—at present my public hears what my characters say, from the characters themselves, and they hear what my characters do, from me; would it not be a directer and more forceful way to let them hear what they say and see what they do? And he concludes that it would be so, and there is the beginning of dramatic art in the artist's mind. Out of this beginning arises the necessity for people to show this action in progress, and the actor's work begins; then a place in which the action may be shown is needed, and a stage is built, and thence we have the whole complicated business of the theatre. In detail we shall find that these new conditions modify or elaborate the nature of narrative art, but in essential significance there is no change. There is a new channel of appeal, a new manner of craftsmanship, but fundamentally the art of drama is the art of simple narrative with the addition of stage action. The spiritual intention and effect of the art of Homer are in kind the same as the spiritual intention and effect of the art of Shakespeare.

I suggest, then, that in principle the practical origin of drama is the instinct of the artist for

## THE NATURE OF DRAMA

widening his audience, and I believe that this is so in actual experience. No man writes plays without the hope, however regularly it may be unrealised, that they will be acted and so reach that wider public that likes to exercise its mind through the use of two senses rather than one. I do not mean that a play can have no existence apart from the stage; it can, and a very vigorous one. But the writer chooses the dramatic form, I believe, with all its difficulties and necessities for compromise, quite definitely with the response of a theatre audience in his mind, and it is for this, and not because of any inherent virtue which he finds in this form and in no other, that his choice is made. The lyrist, the story-teller, the epic poet even, may affect or be truly possessed by an indifference to an audience, but the dramatist is the one literary artist who implicitly accepts the condition, in choosing his form, that the public is his object. He may fulfil this condition triumphantly and with perfect spiritual candour, as the great dramatists have done, but it is in this condition that the whole danger of the theatre lies, as we shall see. One casual consideration may be disposed of here. It is often said—generally by professors in the school of what is ironically called the well-made play—that of all arts the drama is the most difficult. Without supporting the fantastic notion that it is an easier form than the novel because it is a shorter form, I do not believe that it is a greater feat of the imagination to create a great drama than it is to create a great epic, or even, on the grounds of pure creative quality, a great ballad or a great lyric. What is meant, I think, is that when a play is written, and well-written, the mechanical difficulties between the manuscript and a perfect performance are so enormous, the inevitable accidents so many, that the rounded excellence that is comparatively often achieved in the lyric or the ballad or the simple narrative is so hardly achieved in a stage performance as to seem to be almost unattainable, and thus we get an illusion of difficulty, which is really accidental and unrelated to the essential nature of dramatic art.

We may now summarise the distinguishing nature of drama and its evolution thus. The artist to express his emotion needs an image ; looking for one that by its universal relationship shall

# THE NATURE OF DRAMA

bring him a wide hearing, he chooses human character. To display this character he invents an action, and we have the art of narrative. He elaborates or varies his method by appealing not to the ear only of his public but to the ear and eye at once, a place is constructed where this new appeal may be made, and actors are found to make the appeal, and we have the art of the drama and of the theatre. These, simply, would seem to be the conditions of all worthy drama that employs words, conditions with which all worthy drama in the world's literature will be found strictly to comply. And I must now emphasise a point which I have already mentioned more than once, since it is the danger-point which threatens all theatrical ventures and involves many of them in disaster. I have been careful to insist that the image chosen by the truly imaginative artist is human character and that the subsequently invented action is constructed solely as arising out of the natural demands of that character and for the purpose of showing us that character in operation, and never for its own unrelated excitement. So long as this condition is faithfully observed, the dramatist is justified in bringing to his play as much and as exciting action as he can contrive. While an audience whose judgment was not degraded would not complain that *The Medea* was undramatic because it has but little external action, it equally would not resent *Arms and The Man* because it is loaded with it. The dramatist must be free to use as much or as little event as he finds suitable to his intention, but he cannot use event unrelated to character without betraying his honour as an artist. And it is this abuse of event in drama which has vulgarised our English theatre until imaginative and passionate and beautiful work, wrought out of ecstasy and burning with experience, has been very nearly expelled from it altogether. Let us for a moment consider what this action is.

If we take a single normal day in the life of any average being among us, we find that it consists of a series of more or less calculable events, or rather of certain events which belong for the most part to the group of happenings of which experience is common and which we may therefore call calculable, dealt with by that being in the terms of his own individual character. He will, for example, have to go about the earning of his daily bread, he will have to meet and arrange his behaviour towards his family and his friends, he will have to settle with intimates or acquaintances with whom he finds himself in disagreement, he will have to decide how to support the public influences that he conceives to be for good, how to oppose those that he conceives to be for evil, he will have to steel himself against any of the natural losses that may come to him, he will find himself confronted with the beauty and terror of the world and have to come to some reckoning in his soul about them. And when we have seen for a sufficient length of time how he conducts himself in these various and varying but universal relationships, we shall know something—as our insight is keen or weak—of the kind of man he is, of his character. And the dramatist by taking any event or series of events of this kind has a medium through which to show his created persons, fitted to universal experience and understanding, and directly related at all points to that character which is its source and governance in the daily life of the world. For the purposes of his art the artist will select from and heighten these events. He will no more attempt to show us the chaotic and complete action of life than he will attempt to show us the manifold operations of a single character. His business is not to be exhaustive but to be significant. Perceiving some significant aspect of human character, he selects out of the stock of common action an event or events that will serve to give such aspect the opportunity of bringing its significance into tangible shape. It is apparently, from the way in which people talk of the matter, easy to fail to understand how rigorous this selection always is in art. There has, in recent years especially, been a great deal said about the realistic drama, and we are often asked to suppose that what the realistic dramatist gives us is an exact reproduction of the ordinary conduct of daily life. This is nothing but unintelligent nonsense. In this sense, Mr. Galsworthy's *Silver Box* is no more realistic than *Macbeth*, nor, indeed, in any sense. The scenes in the Barthwicks' dining-room are the carefully selected, concentrated and heightened essence of Mr. Galsworthy's knowledge of life, and

# THE NATURE OF DRAMA

could no more take place in the haphazard of an actual dining-room than a Scotch king would actually carry on a conversation with his wife at the supper-table in blank verse. If you used a gramophone and recorded the conversation that passed in two highly critical hours in the lives of three or four people of whom you knew nothing you would find a great deal that was unintelligible, being without its context, a great deal that was wholly irrelevant to the central issue, a great deal of tiresome repetition, a great deal that was inarticulate, all obscuring, if not wholly effacing, the poignant significance at the heart of the matter, and, strictly speaking, it is quite illogical to attempt to put on the stage a photographic reproduction of a room or any other scene as the setting for what, even in the most naturalistic play, is but a conventionalised action. It is the dramatist's business, in the expression of his imaginative vision, to shape this chaos into orderly intelligibility, to give us the context, to strike out the irrelevancies and the reiteration, to say clearly what has been said vaguely, to give proportion where there was none.

We find the dramatist, then, occupied with an aspect of character, going to those normal events which spring from character for the machinery of his drama. But there is another kind of event in life, the event that does not spring from character, or at least does not do so in any way that our human senses can perceive, but is the outcome of accident or unaccountable and negligible eccentricity. An entirely healthy mind has no concern with events of this nature: it spends on them at most but a moment's curiosity. No one with a really healthy and balanced mind, watching, say, a field of haymakers with a river and wooded hills behind, and the sunny clouds of an August day, would trouble to do more than momentarily turn his eyes to see a man on the other side of the hedge standing on his head. And yet, strangely, a man standing on his head can be infallibly certain of drawing a large crowd, and the reason is that we have not, generally speaking, anything like healthy and balanced minds. To support themselves in the monstrous system that has seized upon civilisation, the great majority of men and women have been forced into a way of life that is damned

## THE NATURE OF DRAMA

by a devouring lethargy, which by some strange perversion is called busyness, and in this state all the vital, homely, beautiful events lose their force and delight, and are degraded from what should be hourly significance to sullenly accepted incidents of the daily struggle. And in their place are worshipped the abnormal, the bizarre, the cataclysmic events which will startle jaded susceptibilities into a moment's refreshing activity. A house on fire, a brutal frenzy, a monstrous birth, a sky raining potatoes, a street accident, a man weighing five stone more than he decently ought to, a man who paints bad pictures with his toes, a mirage, snow in July, a leper, a war—these are the things that are infallibly sure of exciting consciousness in a people for whom the sweet and reasonable and common things of the world have grown stale. And out of this miserable condition of life has grown a like condition in the theatre, and one of the great arts of the world has fallen into a disease of which the hideous evidence is on every side of us. Astute business men have observed this condition of our society, and have realised that the demands which it makes can be very readily satisfied in the theatre. And so has come into being a new kind of play, in which character giving rise to action no longer has any place, but in which sensational and abnormal event is of paramount interest. It is a kind of play invented expressly for minds that need an excitement which they can no longer find in nature, that supreme source of excitement when there is sanity to perceive ; for tired minds, for sick minds, for restless and frightened minds, but not for minds that are quiet, vigorous, and eagerly in touch with the simple and normal life that is so marvellously beautiful. Along with this travesty of action in the theatre is a relative travesty of character. The abnormal, the fantastic, the character that is in fact merely an eccentricity—these are the sureties of success, and we have our popular dramatists confessedly depending for motive not upon any profound vision of life quickened through many years of patient and delighted experience, but waiting upon the discovery of some striking situation altogether unrelated to significant life, or of some idiosyncracy that shall masquerade as character instead of being known as the negligible

## THE NATURE OF DRAMA

accident of character. These are the dramatists of occasion, and there is no health in them, but they have infected the theatre, encouraged or commanded by the managers of the theatre, and overrun it with apparently irresistible power. Play after play is produced in London which is modelled exactly to this type. Even if a masterpiece is acted, on the strength of a name as potent as Shakespeare's, it is insolently mauled and hewn precisely in order that this same feverish demand may be satisfied, for when Shakespeare's plays are acted not as the greatest dramatist in the world's history wrote them but as some impertinent producer chooses to rearrange them, it is monstrous to think that the change aims at any heightening of the real dramatic intensity. What it aims at is to throw out the exciting action of the play into undisputed possession of the stage, with the most shameless sacrifice of the character and imaginative passion out of which that action grew in the poet's brain. And from being a device exploited by acute business men for the sake of their purses and an evanescent popularity, this kind of thing has become almost the sole concern of the theatre, and

## PROSE PAPERS

in London, the greatest city of the world, with I know not how many theatres, you may search from end to end of the town and from month to month, and except at an odd half-private performance or two given under crippling difficulties, you will not find any passionate or beautiful work whatever. Here in England we have the finest dramatic literature that any nation has ever produced, and it is neglected in a way which is an unspeakable disgrace. You may mention Granville Barker's Shakespeare revivals, one or two productions at the Frohman Repertory Season, *The Dynasts* at the Kingsway, and I will say that you cannot add six other productions, in the regular course of London theatre management during the last six years, of plays that, as they were produced, have any permanent importance whatever. I say as they were produced, because that rules out practically every Shakespearean revival in the ordinary London theatres other than Mr. Barker's. I do not necessarily say that these lifeless performances, compounded of a cynicism and a sentimentality equally preposterous, should be forbidden the theatre entirely. It may be an

## THE NATURE OF DRAMA

impossible idealism that asks for a society so constituted that there shall be no jaded brains to which this excitement is the only relief; such productions may persist as necessarily as the drug-shops to which Synge likened them. In their place they might be a tolerable nuisance, but the trouble is that they have poisoned our theatres through and through, giving beautiful drama no air that it can breathe, and we have the disgusting spectacle of one theatre manager after another talking of the honourable traditions of the stage while they are battening upon the disease with which they are helping to infest the stage. And sincere dramatic art finds no home among us save at stray performances of a Sunday night club, or when a splendid adventurer like Mr. Poel can bring together the means once in five years to exercise his genius and be called a fanatic for his pains, here and there in enterprise like Sir Frank Benson's company at its prime, or in one or two small provincial theatres, where, as some day will be discovered, dramatic history is being made which is of incomparably more importance than the exploits that engage fashionable attention round about Charing Cross.

Out of its sure knowledge of the needs of a lethargic public imagination, this trade of the theatre has achieved a prosperity in which it is apparently invulnerable. Great capital interests have secured the support of a docile Press, and we have a stupefying condition of things in which the terms " literary drama " has been invented as a term of reproach—as though any verbal drama which was not fine literature also ever has been or could be worth twopence. I would not be unjust about the Press. There are in London two or three critics, and two or three more in the provinces who use a fine intelligence without fear or favour, nor would I be thought to believe that with the more responsible papers good opinion is to be bought. But I do say that the capital power of the commercialised theatre in England to-day is so great that it has been able to impose its standard on nearly all the people who are habitually in contact with its merchandise, and most of the critics among them, so that one piece of catchpenny insincerity after another is extolled by

## THE NATURE OF DRAMA

what passes for expert opinion as a valuable contribution to the great art of the dramatist, while a piece of work like Mr. Gordon Bottomley's *King Lear's Wife*, which, whatever may be questioned in it by the highest standards, is for vigour of imagination, poetic eagerness and dramatic passion not to be excelled by anything that has been put on to the English stage since the Elizabethans, is met with a clamour of ignorance that almost charges the poet with some sinister personal offence, and there is scarcely a theatre critic—the play has been produced twice, and I can remember only one honourable exception—who has either the wit to understand it or the courage to say that he cannot understand it, while in most cases we find no standard whatever being brought to the judgment of an original work of art other than a spurious morality.

Against the return of the theatre to passionate life, then, we have arrayed the condition of our civilisation, a strongly organised and capitalised industry, which is served by highly skilled employees, and bewildered or incapable public guides. The odds are very heavy, and, after some experience of work in the theatre, I believe them to be, from the vaguer visionary's point of view, overwhelmingly heavy. In any widespread reform of the theatre, reaching all this thriving commerce of which we have been speaking, I have little or no faith. Neither this generation nor the next will see the overthrow of a system which is as flourishing as the turf or the business of stocks and shares. To look for a regeneration that shall transform all this expert, prosperous profiteering into the generous and passionate service of art, is but to indulge a pleasant idleness. The only thing to do, if we care about fine drama, and are, nevertheless, determined not to be forbidden the theatre, is to leave this other great organisation happily to its own devices, and do what we can independently of it to satisfy our own needs. If good example should at length affect the whole theatrical body, so much the better, but in the meantime let us give no thought to conscious proselytising, concerning ourselves only with the effort to achieve what we know to be good. With a little courage and a little tolerant patience it can be done. It is wonderful to see how quickly and gratefully the

## THE NATURE OF DRAMA

few people who care deeply for imagination and truth will attach themselves to the most unskilful enterprise if only it be sincere, and it is yet more wonderful to see that sincerity giving skill and mastery to the work, to see the delight of the actor working under these new and vigorous and spiritually exciting conditions, and to see the response of the audience slowly shaping and strengthening itself. There is no more yet to be said to the flourishing trade for which the theatre has been exploited than—you may be secure in the assertion of your will, but you shall no longer dominate ours; you shall have power and notoriety and fat purses in your theatre, but you shall not make it impossible for us to have life in ours.

# ST. JOHN HANKIN

St. John Emile Clavering Hankin died in 1909, at the age of thirty-nine. To discuss the circumstances of his death would be an irrelevancy that could serve no useful purpose. The only word that need be said in this connection is in answer to an ill-considered suggestion that the event was hastened by some sense of disappointment, an unsatisfied hunger for recognition. All artists of real distinction are alike in being proud of their work ; they differ only, for temperamental reasons, in the manner of expressing their pride. Reserve in this matter is not necessarily the virtue of modesty, nor, on the other hand, do we think the less of the makers who have foretold that their rhymes should be more durable than marble monuments. St. John Hankin was proud of his work, and made frank avowal of the fact. " You always think so well of your own plays, Hankin," said a colleague. " Of course I do," was the reply, " otherwise I

## ST. JOHN HANKIN

shouldn't continue to write them." The statement implies no undue self-satisfaction. He was not easily content with the thing he had written, and was a finely conscientious workman in revision and the search for rightness in balance and form. But the task done, he was glad to stand by it, and said so. It is, however, a deep injustice to his memory to suppose that this frankness sprang from any overweening concern for his immediate reputation, and mere folly to add that it affords any clue as to the cause of his last act. In the first place, artists do not die of wounded pride. Keats was not "snuffed out by an article," but by an organic disease, and even Chatterton's tragedy might have been averted by a few shillings a week. Secondly, Hankin had already received a large measure of the only kind of recognition that he valued. He was not forced to write for money, and he neither expected nor wished his plays to be readily accepted by the general public. He was deliberately in the camp of the pioneers, and did not look for the rewards of conformity. But his work had won the approval of progressive audiences, and had been acclaimed by the most liberal critical opinion. The new repertory movement in the theatre, upon which he himself exercised so important an influence, was in turn recognising him as one of its most notable products. His name was one of credit among the people who were seeking to quicken a stage that had grown moribund, and the knowledge that this was so gave him just and genuine pleasure. He was working with a clearly defined aim, and he was achieving his purpose as rapidly as any man can hope to do. St. John Hankin the neglected and disappointed dramatist is a myth. At the time of his death he was winning and enjoying the best kind of success, and his end was one of those untimely accidents of temperament and physical circumstance that we are wise to accept without too curious analysis. Nor would it be profitable to speculate as to what might have been added to his achievement had his life been prolonged. We have to consider his work as it stands, and examine the grounds upon which its claims to permanence may be established.

The decadence of English drama, that began with the passing away of the Elizabethans and has been arrested only in our own day, has commonly been supposed to have been the penalty paid for the neglect of life. By decadence we do not mean a lack of superficial and momentary success. Every age has produced its harvest of plays that would attract and hold large, if uncritical, audiences, and they have not always been wholly bad plays. The great mass of them have, indeed, been radically deficient in true dramatic sense, and, by substituting violent events and action for ideas and character focussed into action, have vulgarised a great art. But a substantial minority have been the product of sincere observation and some feeling for character. And yet, the plays written in England between the end of the Shakesperean age and the beginning of the present generation that are of indisputable excellence when put to the test of the stage and also survive the processes of time might be numbered at a bare dozen ; certainly no more. The Restoration dramatists would contribute some three or four between them ; Goldsmith claims one, perhaps two, Sheridan two, possibly three. The list is not easily to be lengthened. On the other hand, most of the poets of high rank have written plays, and in many cases plays that are immortal, but only by virtue of qualities that are not stage qualities. Action is not essential to the stage, but in its absence there must at least be some direct progression of idea or spiritual conflict that shall perform its office of holding the attention of an audience. The poets have, justly, thrown action from its usurped station in drama, but they have failed either to use it in proper measure or to substitute its equivalent, and for this reason their influence has been deflected from the theatre. We have, then, the few plays that have held the stage and still live; the poets' plays that are imperishable but do not fulfil the requirements of the stage; the large number of plays that sought only a momentary and sensational success and could not, by reason of their essential abuse of dramatic art, achieve more. And there are left those plays, cumulatively through the generations a large number, that had in them some sincerity and conscience and also a measure of fitness for the stage, and have yet passed into oblivion. If we ask ourselves why these plays have perished, we find that the suggestion that the stage had divorced itself from life

## ST. JOHN HANKIN

leaves the question unanswered. The truth is that the stage fell upon evil days not because it divorced itself from life, but because it divorced itself from literature. Literature means style in the expression of life, and if we look at those plays that paid some heed to life and adjusted it with skill to the theatre, we find that the one supreme quality that they lacked is style. The poets have always brought this quality to the drama, but they have neglected the rightful demands of the stage in other things. Drama that shall succeed in the theatre and also be a permanent addition to the art of the world can only spring from the union of an understanding of stage-craft and the faculty of at once seeing and apprehending life and character, or at least manners, and bringing to their expression that discipline of language which is style.

The loftiest style is employed in the service of poetry. When the impulse to express the thing seen passes beyond a certain degree of urgency the expression takes on a new quality of rhythmical force, shaping itself generally into verse. The difference between fine prose and fine verse is fundamentally rather one of urgency, of intensity, than of beauty. The greatest verse may have a loveliness that is not to be found in the greatest prose, but this beauty is a result of the essential distinction, not the distinction itself. It is for this reason that our new drama, full as it is of hope and even achievement, does not yet make any serious challenge to that of the Elizabethans. With two or three exceptions the plays that we have produced have not been forced by the sheer strength of their begetting impulse into poetic form. But many of them have already been so forced into style, a style lower than the highest, but of clear authenticity, and these are plays, too, that are fitted to the requirements of stage presentation. We have not yet regained our lost estate, but we are realising that it is worth regaining, and already the result is a quickening of our dramatic perception. A knowledge of life and the theatre is no longer considered sufficient equipment for the playwright, and men of real literary gifts, men, that is, with the gift of style, are seeking first to understand the theatre so that they may bring their labours to its service. The stage is renewing its old relation to literature, and that is the most wholesome thing that has happened to the stage for nearly three centuries. It was St. John Hankin's privilege and distinction to be one of the first dramatists in England to help in the establishment of this re-union. The great worth of his plays lies not in their philosophy; after all, the Eustace Jacksons of the world have never lacked persuasive and perfectly logical advocates, and Mrs. Cassilis only invents a new trick to emphasise a very old truth. It is not in the technical excellence of their stage-craft; they are often merciless to producer and actors, and St. John Hankin's stage has a habit of resolving itself into a veritable chessboard. They will take a permanent place in the theatre because they are, on the whole and in spite of their flaws in this respect, constructed for action on the stage, and their expression of the dramatist's view of life is vibrant with style from beginning to end.

The distinction between writing that has this quality of style and writing that lacks it, is not the distinction between the same thing well and ill said; it is the distinction between two entirely different things. It is the difference between the dull acceptance which is knowledge and the swift realisation which is imaginative thought. The former might induce a man to speak of one dead as, say, having "escaped from a very worrying world and the annoyances of jealous and unjust people and the disappointments of life in general," but it is clearly a mistake to suppose that he experiences or expresses the same spiritual emotion as the man who cries out :

> He has outsoared the shadow of our night ;
> Envy and calumny and hate and pain,
> And that unrest which men miscall delight
> Can touch him not and torture not again ;
> From the contagion of the world's slow stain
> He is secure, and now can never mourn
> A heart grown cold, a head grown grey in vain ;
> Nor when the spirit's self has ceased to burn
> With sparkless ashes load an unlamented urn.

The difference here is that between formal assent and vision. Ultimately it is sincerity that creates style, and sincerity has been lost to our theatre save for brief interludes until these new dramatists once again began to write not from rumour but from conscience. Those momentarily successful plays that presented life not altogether distorted and at the same time fulfilled the technical requirements of the stage perished because their virtues were not really sincere. Their makers said the right thing because it was commonly reported to be the right thing and not from conviction, and consequently said it ill, which, artistically, amounted to not saying it at all. Lacking the sincerity which should result in style, they lacked the power of complete utterance, and in art a thing either is completely said or it does not exist. We must not, of course, confuse completeness with over-elaboration; reticence is often the spirit of style. Completeness implies the embodiment of the creative ecstasy of the artist with the actual statement made, and this ecstasy cannot exist, of course, apart from the strictest sincerity.

Among the many vague generalities that have gained currency among us none is more thoughtless than the pronouncement that art should imitate nature. It should do nothing of the sort. When Oscar Wilde asserted that, on the contrary, nature imitates art, he was only refuting what he knew to be a shallow conventionalism with his usual fantastic gaiety. It would need a good deal of ingenious sophistry for such an ideal to find a more excellent realisation than the photograph and the gramophone. Nature—life—becomes art only by concentration and selection. A play focusses into two hours the selected and concentrated experience of many lives, and it finds an expression that is correspondingly artificial and purged. Its failure to do this is the measure of its failure as a work of art. It is for this reason that the greatest drama is the poetic drama, where the expression reaches the highest artificiality, and the symbol most consistently takes the place of the traditional formula of speech. To say that a play is true to life, in the sense that it is an unshaped extract from life, and that its people speak in lifelike speech, is utterly to condemn it. Those plays of which I have spoken frequently preserved, when they were not couched in fustian rhetoric, the most exact parallel to the daily use of conversation. The point is that in either case they were the result of hearsay and not of imagination ; they accepted without question either the false rumours of literature which their authors had never examined or

## ST. JOHN HANKIN

the current speech of daily life which had lost all freshness and a great deal of its meaning. Ibsen paused to consider this question before making his plays, or perhaps it would be nearer the truth to say that, bringing real creative impulse to his work, he necessarily rejected at the outset the false doctrines of common acceptance. St. John Hankin was one of the men who, consciously or not, profited by the example. His characters are as far removed as possible in expression from a debased tradition of literary grandiosity, and, on the other hand, they are far from reaching high imaginative utterance. But their speech is, nevertheless, definitely one of the imagination:

HENRY.—It was extremely undignified and quite unnecessary. If you had simply come up to the front door and rung the bell you would have been received just as readily.

EUSTACE.—I doubt it. In fact, I doubt if I should have been received at all. I might possibly have been given a bed for the night, but only on the distinct understanding that I left early the next morning. Whereas now nobody talks of my going. A poor invalid! In the doctor's hand! Perfect quiet essential. No. My plan was best.

HENRY.—Why didn't that fool Glaisher see through you?

EUSTACE.—Doctors never see through their patients.

## PROSE PAPERS

It's not what they're paid for, and it's contrary to professional etiquette. (*Henry snorts wrathfully*.) Besides, Glaisher's an ass, I'm glad to say.

HENRY (*fuming*).—It would serve you right if I told the Governor the whole story.

EUSTACE.—I daresay. But you won't. It wouldn't be cricket. Besides, I only told you on condition you kept it to yourself.

HENRY (*indignant*).—And so I'm to be made a partner in your fraud. The thing's a swindle, and I've got to take a share in it.

EUSTACE.—Swindle? Not a bit. You've lent a hand—without intending it—to reuniting a happy family circle. Smoothed the way for the Prodigal's return. A very beautiful trait in your character.

HENRY (*grumpy*).—What I don't understand is why you told me all this. Why in heaven's name didn't you keep the whole discreditable story to yourself?

EUSTACE (*with flattering candour*).—The fact is I was pretty sure you'd find me out. The Governor's a perfect owl, but you've got brains—of a kind. You can see a thing when it's straight before your nose. So I thought I'd let you into the secret from the start, just to keep your mouth shut.

HENRY.—Tck! (*thinks for a moment*). And what are you going to do now you are at home?

EUSTACE (*airily*).—Do, my dear chap? Why, nothing.

(*And on the spectacle of Eustace's smiling self-assurance and Henry's outraged moral sense, the curtain falls.*)

That is not the speech of daily life. No two brothers ever talked to each other or could talk so.

## ST. JOHN HANKIN

There is in their conversation something added to the actual argument between the two men, and this addition is Hankin's imagination. Eustace and Henry Jackson are not wholly creatures of their own independent being; they exist partly in terms of their creator's temperament and vision, and they justly and inevitably bear witness to this fact in their utterance. The philosophy that finds a spark of the Godhead in every man is relatively applicable to art. The creature bears in him some token of the creator, and unless he does so he is deprived of his proudest right. The dramatist whose characters are set out photographically, not reflected through the distinctive medium of his own personality, does not create at all and he has no claim to consideration as an artist. He may then catch the verisimilitude of speech, but the spirit with which he should invest words must necessarily be beyond his consciousness, and his expression will remain untranslated into style.

It is a curious fact that this essential condition of all art should have been so often overlooked in dramatic criticism whilst its importance has been consistently recognised in the discussion of the other arts. A poem or a picture or a statue is accounted as deficient in the finer parts of its being unless it bears in its composition some signature of its source, and yet for some obscure reason we have been asked to consider it as a virtue that a play should be as a bough lopped from the tree of life, unshaped and showing no pressure of the artist's hand. The great dramatists have never bestowed their approval on this monstrous notion by their practice. The art of the dramatist is, indeed, more essentially objective than that of his fellows, but objectivity in art does not imply an abortive dissociation of the thing seen from the eyes that see. Strangely enough, St. John Hankin, who realised this truth always in his art, appeared to lend support to its violation in an essay otherwise full of admirable reason. " It is the dramatist's business," he says, " to represent life, not to argue about it." It is, perhaps, not special pleading to suggest that in speaking of argument he had in mind the distortion of life to make it conform to fore-ordained ends. The sentence is to be found in the *Note on Happy Endings*, where he justly resents the sentimental intrusion of expediency on the dramatist's conception of truth. His protest would seem to be made rather against the sophistical devices of argument than against argument in the shape of commentary, but, with so important an issue at stake, he would have done well to have considered his statement more carefully. However this may be, it is clear that all dramatists who have written sincerely have not only represented life, but argued about it. The very texture of their expression, as in the passage that has been quoted, is an implicit argument about life, in that it knits up the artist's temperament into the speech of his characters. But the argument has always been explicit also, a deliberate as well as an incidental commentary. The Greek chorus was, fundamentally, a device employed by the poet whereby he might exercise this privilege of argument. The characters that he created might be allowed to work out their own destiny as far as he could enable them to do so by virtue of his experience of life; but he was careful to reserve his right of commentary upon the process. The æsthetic value of this determination is obvious. Our demand of the artist is that he should show us not life, but his vision of life. The earliest English drama made frank allowance of this right, an allowance too frank, indeed, to be artistically sound. The explicit argument was not clearly cut off from the characterisation as it had been by the Greeks, nor was it yet woven into the fibre of the characterisation in the manner attempted by the Elizabethans. And the Elizabethans themselves were not blameless in this matter. In rejecting the classical model Shakespeare set himself the most difficult of his technical problems. His magnificent genius justified its own choice, but the soliloquy was, inherently, a less perfect artistic form than the chorus. The greatest difficulty in the loyal presentation of Shakespeare's plays is in dealing convincingly with these choric soliloquies. To adopt the line of least resistance and cut them out, as is commonly done, is merely to maim the poet. Shakespeare felt the artistic necessity of comment upon his creations, but in blurring the dividing line between his dramatic and choric statement instead of defining it sharply he deprived his audience of help to which it has a legitimate claim. But difficulty is no excuse for inefficiency, and no Shakesperean production is of the slightest æsthetic value that does not honestly seek to meet the difficulty instead of evading it.

The demands of art upon the artist are inexorable. The artist finds certain requirements imposed upon him by his work from which there is no escape. And one of these is this necessity of the chorus, or the poet's argument in drama. The whole significance of the chorus in the drama of the theatre had fallen into neglect and oblivion, because the plays of the theatre were being written by men who had no sincerity of artistic impulse. And then, as soon as men once more bring their conscience to this work and write sincerely as artists, we find the necessity reasserting itself in spite of any reasoned denial. The new dramatists, of whom St. John Hankin was one of the ablest and sincerest, seemed to be determined that the construction of their plays should follow a false tradition at least in this, that it should not allow anything to interfere with the development of the action. But they were too good artists to be able to carry out their own determination. Being sincere, and creating characters instead of cutting them out with a pair of scissors, they found it necessary, as we have seen, to invest them with something of their own temper, and that in itself wholesomely disturbed the mechanical continuity that had become a fetish. Here was the beginning of regeneration, and the beginning forced its own growth. Having brought implicit argument back to the drama, they felt an artistic desire for argument that was explicit. Not being quite sure of themselves, they refrained from satisfying the desire openly, and they started a new tradition, which will, it is safe to prophesy, prove nothing more than the prelude to a return to the frank acceptance of an essential artistic necessity. They invented the stage direction. Not the old direction that set out a stage and brought people on to it and off again, but a new full-bodied thing that enabled them to do something which their art compelled them to do.

GENERAL BONSOR (*too broken with the world's ingratitude to protest further*).—Boring ! (*follows Miss Triggs, shaking his poor old head. There is a pause while we realise that one of the most tragic things in life is to be a bore—and to know it. Mrs. Eversleigh, however, not being cursed with the gift*

## ST. JOHN HANKIN

*of imaginative sympathy, wastes no pity on the General. Instead of this she turns to her sister, and, metaphorically speaking, knocks her out of the ring.)*

That is pure chorus, and nothing else. And again :

> MRS. JACKSON.—But what became of your money, dear ? The thousand pounds your father gave you ?
> EUSTACE.—I lost it.
> MRS. JACKSON (*looking vaguely round as if Eustace might have dropped it somewhere on the carpet, in which case, of course, it ought to be picked up before someone treads on it.*) Lost it ?

This is as clear in intention as a chorus of Trojan women, and instances are to be found on nearly every page of the authentic artists who are re-establishing the credit of our theatre. They are, indeed, to be found on the pages only, not yet on the stage in their complete and rightful authority, but the fact that they are conceived and written is evidence of the return of a perfectly sound instinct. The most complete attempts to give this elemental desire natural expression that have yet been made in modern drama are, perhaps, to be found in certain of Mr. Yeats's plays and in the Gaffer of Mr. Masefield's *Nan*.

*The Two Mr. Wetherbys* was written in 1902.

# PROSE PAPERS

Before that date St. John Hankin had worked as dramatic and literary critic, and was known as a contributor to *Punch*. He had by him, too, the usual sheaf of plays, and was wise enough to leave them in their pigeon-holes when his reputation as a dramatist might have lent them a value not their own. He looked upon *The Two Mr. Wetherbys* as the first achievement by which he cared to stand. *Mr. Punch's Dramatic Sequels* was published in 1901, but its wit is relatively immature and not comparable with that of his *Lost Masterpieces*, published three years later. Between 1902 and his death he wrote seven plays and began an eighth, and it is upon these that his reputation rests. In *The Two Mr. Wetherbys* certain of his qualities appear almost in their full development, others scarcely at all. The faculty of writing dialogue, the style, the salty wit and the debonair, faintly cynical philosophy of life, are all there. But there is as yet nothing of the deeper humour and the real tenderness that were to throw their gracious charity over the mocking satire of the later plays, nor is the artistic sincerity yet perfect. It is the only one of his plays that has a conventionally happy ending of the kind that he laughed at so vigorously in the preface from which I have already quoted, and it is the only one that ends unsatisfactorily. In sending Dick and Constantia off to inevitable domestic tribulation, he may have had his tongue in his cheek; but, if so, the humour was too subtle to be safe, involving as it did a direct negation of his own conviction. The whole question of the destiny of the artists' creations is necessarily one that each artist must decide for himself. St. John Hankin quite rightly decided that the romantic conclusions popularly favoured were false. It does not follow that they are false to life or to another artist's view of life, but simply that they were false for him. They are, indeed, commonly enough so contrived as to fail altogether in artistic conviction, but this does not affect their radical fitness when conceived by the right temperament. Eustace Jackson's engagement to Stella Farringford would, doubtless, have trebled the popularity of *The Return of the Prodigal*, but any balance in our knowledge of life, or, more particularly, in our knowledge of Hankin's vision of life, precludes us from deploring his refusal to sanction such an event; but we are, none the less, profoundly disturbed by the accident that prevents the consummation of Romeo's love for Juliet. It is the prerogative of passion to take no account of institutions or social expediency. Great poets in their most passionate seasons create without reference to anything save their own burning conception. Love's moment is for them an immortal term which is independent of any subsequent reaction or retribution. But it was Hankin's limitation as an artist that he could not see life detached from such institutions and expediencies. He could see clearly, but not very deeply; his characters are alive and considered from many points of view, but he was never able to divest them of the rags of circumstance. The danger of passion was, in consequence, a more real thing for him than its glory. Much as he did for the renascence of drama in many ways, he was yet far from bringing reason under the fine subjection of the imagination. Eustace's marriage to Stella would have been a catastrophe only because these peoples were created by Hankin's temperament; a greater imagination might have made such an event

## ST. JOHN HANKIN

triumphant. An artist, however, is not to be censured for his limitations, but only for his refusal to recognise and work within them. Of the higher things of passion Hankin was incapable, but he was wisely content to acknowledge the incapacity, and, working consistently within his powers, he rediscovered certain artistic principles of first-rate importance, in the expression of an impulse not of the highest order, yet in itself of no mean value.

*The Return of the Prodigal*, which followed the *Wetherbys*, was written in 1904. Not only have the qualities that were found in the earlier play matured, but there are new qualities discovered. If it was not given to him to be passionate, Hankin here shows that he could encompass a quite rare tenderness. Mrs. Jackson, first-cousin to the Lady Denison of a later date, is conceived with a charity that has in it no trace of cynicism. She is not a central figure in the play, and yet she is, it seems to me, more completely imagined than any other character in the whole of Hankin's work. This is not to say that she is the most striking of his people, but there is in her just that subtlety of presentment that is the product not of deliberation but of uncurbed artistic instinct. She is there for no other purpose than to satisfy the dramatist's impulse to embody a type for which he clearly had no common affection. Eustace and Henry, Samuel Jackson and even his daughter Violet, admirably fashioned as they are, are yet moved by a purpose that is not wholly their own, and answer in some measure to the dictates of the dramatist's reason. But Mrs. Jackson is a complete creation, arguing nothing, doing nothing, merely being, and in her Hankin approaches poetic imagination in conception, though not in utterance. And it is noteworthy that, moving on this higher artistic plane, her influence upon the other characters of the play is more authentically dramatic than is that commonly operating between Hankin's people. The conflict between Eustace and his father and brother is, again, primarily one of the reasons, just as, in a lesser degree, is that between him and his sister. They have a definite and circumstantial problem to solve, and they argue the matter out consistently in terms of their own personalities. But Eustace's relation to his mother is an emotional one, and, consequently, far more moving. "Dear old mater. She's not clever, but for real goodness of heart I don't know her equal." Speaking of her he becomes, for a moment, greater than himself, concerned with simple and fundamental and not complex and superficial things.

In 1905 two plays were written, *The Charity that Began at Home* and *The Cassilis Engagement*. If Hankin saw life in something less than heroic proportions, he was at least able to apply an almost faultless logic to the life that he did see. His world was circumscribed, but he purged it thoroughly of shams, and if to do this is not the highest function of the artist it is one of the most worthy functions of the artist who professes no kinship with the greatest. And it is certainly to be accounted to him artistically as a virtue that although he exposed what he considered to be ethical and social fallacies in some measure by statement and argument, he did so in a larger measure by the operation of character. In other words, although he intuitively realised the necessity of the chorus in drama, he was also able to preserve a just balance between chorus and action. The questions that confront Lady Denison and Mrs. Cassilis are considered by the dramatist not only with fine subtlety and mental precision, but also with a quite notable instinct for dramatic form. Generally speaking, the impulse behind the plays is not sufficiently imaginative to raise them save at rare intervals to the level of a Mrs. Jackson, but the instinct that directed the adjustment of the relations of the dramatist's reflections to the action of his characters was in nearly every case sound. Whilst the dramatist may and should argue about life, it is not his business to argue about ideas in the abstract. If he uses his characters merely as mouthpieces for the exploitation of abstractions he abuses them; his privilege of choric commentary is justly exercised only when it is confined to the contemplation of ideas that shape themselves out of the action of his characters; when, in other words, it is applied to the general only as it is resolved from the particular. It is not for Œdipus, crushed, blind and bereft, driven from his fellows, to be conscious of more than his immediate misery; life, for him, has become the present moment of fierce pain and nothing more. But the

## ST. JOHN HANKIN

poet, seeing his creation set against the whole of experience, remembering this man's beginning and story and all men's hope, can draw from the disastrous moment an abstract idea purged into peace, almost into exultation:

> Ye citizens of Thebes, behold; 'tis Œdipus that passeth here,
> Who read the riddle-word of Death, and mightiest stood of mortal men,
> And Fortune loved him, and the folk that saw him turned and looked again.
> Lo, he is fallen, and around great storms and the out-reaching sea!
> Therefore, O man, beware and look toward the end of things that be,
> The last of sights, the last of days, and no man's life account as gain
> Ere the full tale be finished and the darkness find him without pain.[1]

Hankin was not a poet and did not move upon these emotional planes, but within the limits of

---

[1] Professor Gilbert Murray's translation. It is a striking commentary upon the common confusion as to the æsthetic meaning of the choric element in drama that in a recent production of *Œdipus Rex* in this country these last lines which, when spoken, as Sophocles directed, by the chorus, have an emotional value scarcely to be paralleled in dramatic poetry, were allotted to Œdipus himself, and so deprived of every vestige of significance.

his own less ambitious design his instinct guided him to a proportion in this matter that was perfectly just, and he helped definitely towards a new understanding of one of the subtlest principles of dramatic form.

*The Last of the De Mullins* was written in 1907 and was Hankin's last dramatic work save two one-act plays and an unfinished comedy. The sociological problem which is its theme is set out with his customary lucidity and investigated fairly in terms of art and not of propaganda. Great passion in art is, always, the product of the imagination, and yet it is in this play which is further away from imagination than any other of his more important efforts, that he approaches most nearly to passion. The reason is that Hankin's imagination being the least developed of his qualities, the problems of reason which he explored depended for their power of moving him deeply upon the directness with which they were stated. The social question of Janet De Mullin is more complete and clearly stated than those of Mrs. Cassilis and Geoffrey, of Lady Denison or Eustace Jackson. However improbable it may be, it is remotely

## ST. JOHN HANKIN

possible that an adjustment of circumstances might show Mrs. Cassilis to be mistaken, Lady Denison to be wise in her charity, and the Jackson compromise to be something other than the best possible solution of the family conflict. This is not to suggest that Hankin should have resolved these plays in any way other than that he chose, but to point out that in each instance it might be urged that he controlled the conduct of his protagonists to certain ends, and that other ends are conceivable. But Janet's attitude and conduct are inevitable, and her decisions are the only ones that we could accept as being possible. And this tightening up of his reasoning faculty served Hankin for the moment in some measure as a substitute for imaginative intensity and brought him near to passion. Janet is the one figure among his men and women of whom we can think as loving passionately and being passionately loved.

The new seriousness of *The Last of the De Mullins* precluded any free exercise of the wit that had been so admirably employed in the earlier plays, but otherwise his qualities here reach their full maturity. The mastery of style has developed, and the characterisation has gained in subtlety and the power of suggestion. Mrs. De Mullin may be set beside Lady Denison and Mrs. Jackson, and De Mullin himself, choleric and stiff-necked as he is, bears witness anew to the tenderness with which his creator contemplated the foibles and prejudices of his creations. It was a rare gift of Hankin's, one that has been memorable in many greater men, this faculty of making human weakness at least not contemptible. There is scarcely a noble figure in his plays—even Violet Jackson lacks something of courage—and yet there is scarcely one for whom we cannot spare some affection. Lady Farringford herself might discover a heart at any moment.

The two one-act plays, *The Burglar Who Failed* and *The Constant Lover*, were both written in 1908. The former is an amiable little farce, not unpleasing, but far from showing the dramatist at his best. It has an air of being manufactured. But *The Constant Lover* is one of the most perfectly polished excursions in prose comedy dialogue that the new drama has produced. Conceived with a fancy of

## ST. JOHN HANKIN

quite uncommon delicacy, the play is carried through from the first word to the last without a flaw. It is full of good sunshine and laughter, light and debonair yet wholly sincere. Hankin never realised his aim more fully than in this little masterpiece, and although it stands of necessity below his more ambitious work in many ways it is, perhaps, a more perfect achievement than anything else that he did. He himself valued it highly, and the last letter he ever wrote closed with a reference to it, poignant and yet not without cheer.

When he died Hankin left an unfinished play, *Thompson*. He had written the first act and some later fragments. Relying far more upon a conventional and definite plot than was his custom, it was clearly his intention to give free rein in the dialogue to the wit of which he was a master. Mr. George Calderon's able completion of an extremely difficult task must speak for itself. In addition to his plays Hankin wrote a number of essays on the theatre which, apart from the excellence of their matter, are remarkable for their admirable prose.

## PROSE PAPERS

As in the plays, imaginative beauty is beyond the writer's aim, but there is always a clear-cut precision, a lucidity and balance of statement, that are a lasting delight even when the subject under discussion is not of permanent interest or the point of view has become obsolete.

But when the Puritan stayed away from the theatre altogether, irrespective of the character of the play presented, his approval or disapproval became a matter of indifference to the management. It is very gratifying, of course, when you put up a play, to have it praised by the godly for its elevating tendency. But if none of the godly will come to see it your only course is to withdraw it and substitute something to attract the wicked. For the wicked, with all their faults, buy seats. And so the drama, which, like the rest of the arts, is in its essence neither moral nor immoral, neither religious nor irreligious, got a bad name, and when a calling, or an art, or an institution gets a bad name it soon begins to deserve it.

That is a fair example of the style employed in these essays, and it would be difficult to find a higher excellence in the same province.

In these occasional papers Hankin makes many shrewd observations upon his art and allows us many entertaining glimpses of his philosophy in the rough, of the materials in his workshop. How suggestive, for example, in the light of the plays, is that passage in the essay on "Mr. Bernard Shaw as Critic," where he slyly opposes his own spirit of comedy to the rather dour gravity that he was one of the few men wise enough to find in his subject. Quoting a paragraph from Mr. Shaw's *Dramatic Opinions*, he comments: "This is not the voice of a jester. It is the voice of Dr. Clifford," and proceeds:

Again, of Miss Mary Anderson's autobiography he writes—

"Note how she assumes, this girl who thinks she has been an artist, that the object of going on the stage is to sparkle in the world and that the object of life is happiness!"

One can almost hear the thump on the cushion as the preacher utters that sentence. Yet I fancy most people have been in the habit of regarding Mr. Shaw's attitude towards the theatre as one of flippant tolerance largely tinged with contempt. The republication of these criticisms should serve to correct that impression. One would rather like to hear, by the way, what the "object of life" really is from Mr. Shaw's point of view. Perhaps some day he will write a play about it.

St. John Hankin lived and wrote at the beginning of a new movement, and his permanent distinction in drama will be rather that of right endeavour and the recapture of just instincts than of full-bodied achievement. But that his plays have durable qualities there is no question. They are a valuable effort towards the re-establishment of the union between drama and literature; they contain at least a suggestion of a return to true principles of dramatic form; they have not style in its rarer manifestation, but they have style, and that is much. Hankin's characters are not very passionately conceived nor are they stirred often by the essential emotions of men, but they have life. The comedy which is Falstaff can stale only with the change of fundamental humanity: the comedy which is Eustace Jackson might lose some of its flavour with a change of certain social conditions; Eustace is, nevertheless, a quick creation and not a puppet. The *Note on Happy Endings* pleasantly emphasises the fine objectivity with which the dramatist saw his characters. In bringing them into existence he gave them also independence of being, and is able seriously to discuss their future and their problems of conduct with as much detach-

## ST. JOHN HANKIN

ment as he would gossip of his neighbours over the tea-cups. In the essay on Mr. Shaw he gives counsel to critics that is peculiarly valuable in the consideration of his own plays:

> Our dramatic critic, as a class, are always asking whether the dramatist is doing what *they* want, instead of giving their minds to the only question of any importance critically, namely, whether he has done what *he* wants, and done it competently.

And done it competently. That is the point. It does not follow that even if he has done this we shall like his work, but in that event it is better to leave it alone than to denounce it for not being something else. Swinburne was not far wide of the mark when he said that the only criticism of value was the criticism that praised. Those of us who believe that the stage cannot regain its full vigour until it has rediscovered poetry as its natural expression, find in Hankin and his three or four adventurous fellows invigorating promise rather than fulfilment, but we are foolish if we refuse gratitude to the men who have made the first step towards the new estate and deny ourselves the pleasure that their work can give.

## PROSE PAPERS

Among these men Hankin takes an honourable place, and that he was one of the few who first sought to bring back sincerity and a fit dignity of form to a great art is a distinction that will not easily stale.

**OHIO UNIVERSITY LIBRARY**

Please return this book as soon as you have finished with it. In order to avoid a fine it must be returned by the latest date stamped below.

MAR 30 1998

MAR 1 2 1998

CF